Twayne's English Authors Series

EDITOR OF THIS VOLUME

Arthur F. Kinney

University of Massachusetts

Henry Peacham

TEAS 251

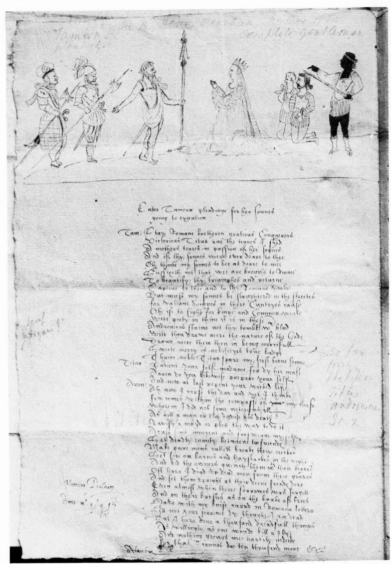

HENRY PEACHAM

By ALAN R. YOUNG

Acadia University

TWAYNE PUBLISHERS
A DIVISION OF G. K. HALL & CO., BOSTON

Copyright © 1979 by G. K. Hall & Co.
Published in 1979 by Twayne Publishers,
A Division of G. K. Hall & Co.
All Rights Reserved

Printed on permanent/durable acid-free paper and bound
in the United States of America

First Printing

Frontispiece illustration: Shakespeare's *Titus Andronicus* in Performance (1595). Manuscript in the library of the Marquess of Bath at Longleat (Harley Papers, Vol. I, fol. 159). The leaf is signed "Henricus Peacham" in the lower left corner.

Library of Congress Cataloging in Publication Data

Young, Alan R   1941–
Henry Peacham.

(Twayne's English Authors series; TEAS 251)
Bibliography: p. 157–62
Includes index.
1. Peacham, Henry, 1576?–1643?—Criticism and
interpretation.
PR2329.P15Z98   828'.3'09   78-13240
ISBN 0-8057-6732-0

Contents

About the Author

Alan R. Young was born in England in 1941. After completing his B.A. at the University of Bristol he worked as a Government Education Officer in East Africa and then moved permanently to Canada. He has taught at Simon Fraser University and the University of Alberta and completed a Ph.D. at this latter institution in 1970. He is currently an Associate Professor in the Department of English at Acadia University. In 1976–77 he was Longman Visiting Fellow in the Institute of Bibliography and Textual Criticism at the University of Leeds. His scholarly interests are divided between English Renaissance literature and Canadian literature. His publications include a book on the Canadian novelist Ernest Buckler, introductions to editions of Henry Peacham's *Emblemata Varia* and two novels by Ernest Buckler, and numerous articles and reviews in such publications as the *Dalhousie Review, English Studies in Canada, History Today, Journal of Canadian Fiction, Studies in English Literature,* and the *University of Toronto Quarterly.*

Preface

The name Henry Peacham is primarily associated by students of the seventeenth century with two important treatises on the graphic arts, with one of the most important English collections of emblems, with two lively collections of epigrams, with a group of essays and pamphlets on a wide variety of topical issues, and above all with the best-known work of courtesy literature of the period, that magnificent compendium of the earlier Renaissance ideals of gentlemanly upbringing, that is aptly called *The Compleat Gentleman*. Due to the breadth of subject-matter that Peacham's works cover, his name is familiar not just to students of literature but also to those of the fine arts, music, education, and social history. In spite of his importance to a number of scholarly disciplines, however, no comprehensive study of his works has ever been published.[1] The present study will attempt to survey all of Peacham's writings and to evaluate their place in English letters. Many of Peacham's works have never received any detailed discussion in print before, and I have often been conscious that a survey of the kind given here will inevitably fall short of comprehensiveness in its details because of the necessary limitations of space.

Peacham continues to be recognized primarily as the author of a classic of courtesy literature, but appreciation of his other writings is growing. This is in part due to current interest in emblem literature which has revealed the full extent of his contribution to that most characteristic of Renaissance art forms. In an important article F. J. Levy has drawn attention also to Peacham's concern with the graphic arts. Recently, too, Robert Cawley's book on Peacham's poetry has provided a reminder of this especially neglected aspect of his work. Finally, Harold Levitt, in his doctoral dissertation on Peacham's political writings, has raised intriguing questions about Peacham's participation in the political and religious pamphleteering that was so intense in the seventeenth century in the years leading up to the Civil War.[2]

In the pages that follow I will, of course, discuss Peacham's contribution to both courtesy and emblem literature, but I hope also to offer an exploration of Peacham's other writings and convey a sense of their versatility and quality. No one who reads *The Truth of Our Times, Thalia's Banquet, A Merry Discourse of Meum and Tuum,* or *The Art of Living in London,* for example, can fail to be impressed by the vitality of Peacham's handling of language, his humor and incisive wit, his gift for the concise anecdote, and, in an age given to extremes, his remarkable moderation. He once declared that ". . . all the errors that men commit in their whole lives, is for want of the line and levell of an eaven and true judgment,"[3] and it is this view, one senses, that permitted him to be more clear-sighted than most about the tumultuous events of his age, making him today one of its most attractive representatives.

Acknowledgments

In the course of my research for this study of Henry Peacham I have incurred many debts to individuals and institutions. Most particularly I wish to thank Dr. John Horden, Director of the Institute of Bibliography and Textual Criticism at the University of Leeds for his enthusiastic encouragement and scholarly advice; Allan Gilbert, Professor Emeritus at Duke University, for some invaluable suggestions concerning Peacham's sources; and Margaret Vincent (formerly Pitman), who made her M.A. thesis and subsequent research notes on Peacham freely available to me along with the hospitality of her home. To Acadia University I am indebted for a Sabbatical Leave during which much of this book was written, and to the Canada Council I am indebted for a generous Leave Fellowship that provided the necessary financial support. I also wish to record my warmest appreciation to the publishing firm of Longman which endowed the position of Longman Visiting Fellow in the Institute of Bibliography at the University of Leeds. My year's stay as Longman Fellow at Leeds was an opportunity as enjoyable as it was fruitful, and the pages of this book owe much to the research and writing I was able to carry out there. Finally I wish to acknowledge the generous assistance I invariably received from the staff of the many libraries and record offices which I visited in the course of my research. I especially thank the staff at the Bodleian Library, the British Library, Chetham's Library, the Folger Shakespeare Library, the Guildhall Library of London, the Hertfordshire Record Office, the Lincolnshire County Archives, the Norfolk Record Office, and the Public Record Office.

Chronology

1578   Henry Peacham born at North Mymms, Hertfordshire. Son of Henry Peacham (1547–1634), author of *The Garden of Eloquence* (1577), and Anne (née Fairclough). Educated at schools near St. Albans and in London.

1592   Matriculated as sizar at Trinity College, Cambridge.

1595   Graduated B.A. from Cambridge. Sketch of performance (or rehearsal) of a scene from Shakespeare's *Titus Andronicus*.

1598   Graduated M.A. from Cambridge. At about this time may have visited Modena to study music under Orazio Vecchi to whom he refers in *The Compleat Gentleman* as "mine owne Master."

1600   From about 1600 to 1607 was schoolmaster at Kimbolton School, Huntingdonshire.

1603   Presented James I with some of his emblems in Huntingdon (April 27–29). At about the same time composed the music and words of his madrigal "Awake softly with singing Oriana sleeping." Between March, 1603, and 20 October, 1604 composed a manuscript emblem book, *Basilicon Doron*, which he dedicated to James I. Another copy (not now extant) presented to the King.

1606   *The Art of Drawing* (another issue in 1607).

1607   Appears to have moved to London.

1608   *The More the Merrier*. Gives address as Fetter Lane, London. Sometime before 1612 moved to St. Martin's-in-the-Fields Parish, Westminster.

1610   Third *Basilicon Doron* manuscript emblem book, dedicated and presented to Prince Henry. Contributed dedicatory poem for Robert Dowland's *A Musical Banquet*. At about this time present at Court where he frequently drew "his Maiesties" portrait.

1611   Dedicatory poem for Arthur Standish's *The Commons Complaint*. Dedicatory emblem and poems for Thomas Coryate's *Coryats Crudities*.

1612   Baptism of daughter Sara in St. Martin's-in-the-Fields Parish Church (27 April). *Minerva Britanna* (signed from

Richmond). *Graphice* (also issued with alternate title *The Gentleman's Exercise*). Watercolor portrait of Prince Henry for James Cleland's manuscript "Le Povrtraict de Monseigneur le Prince."

1613   *The Period of Mourning* and *Nuptiall Hymnes*. Begins journey to France, Germany, and Low Countries.

1614   With Sir John Ogle, Governor of Utrecht. With army in Low Countries from 7 September to 9 October. At Breda after Treaty of Xanten (November).

1615   Between November, 1614, and 18 January, 1615 returned to England. *A Most True Relation* and *Prince Henrie Revived*. 10 March Edmund Peacham attempts to implicate him while being tried for treason.

1615   Schoolmaster at Wymondham, Norfolk, until 1620.

1620   Shortly after 17 August makes acquaintance in Norwich of William Howard, son of Earl of Arundel, and between 1620 and 1622 makes acquaintance of Richard Sackville, Third Earl of Dorset. *Thalia's Banquet.*

1621   At about this time schoolmaster in St. Martin's-in-the-Fields. Completes manuscript emblem book *Emblemata Varia*, which he dedicates to Sir Julius Caesar.

1622   *The Compleat Gentleman* (signed "from my house at Hogsdon by London").

1623   Baptism in Boston, Lincolnshire, of "Elizabeth d. Henrie Peacham" (November 13).

1624   *An Aprill Shower*. Working as a schoolmaster in Boston.

1627   *The Compleat Gentleman* (2nd edition).

1629   Frances Rich, Countess of Warwick, asks Peacham to design for her a monument to be erected in Snarford Church, Lincolnshire, at her death.

1632   Replaces John Bedford for three years on temporary basis as schoolmaster at Heighington Free School, Lincolnshire.

1634   *Thestylis Atrata. The Compleat Gentleman* (3rd edition). *The Gentleman's Exercise* (2nd edition).

1636   *Coach and Sedan*. Marriage Licence Allegation (November 11) referring to Henry Peacham, clerk, of Chelsea, widower aged 50, and Ann Emmerson, widow, aged 60, of St. Martin's-in-the-Fields (possibly the same man as the subject of this study).

1637   Poems for two engravings by Wenceslaus Hollar: "Seleucus and Son" and "Greenwich."

1638   *The Valley of Varietie* and *The Truth of Our Times.*

1639   *The Duty of All True Subjects* and *A Merry Discourse of Meum and Tuum.* Poem for Hollar engraving: Diptych of "Richard II and Virgin and Child."

1641   *The Worth of a Peny* and *A Dialogue between the Crosse in Cheap, and Charing Crosse.* Poems for Hollar engravings: "En Surculus Arbor" and "The World is Ruled and Governed by Opinion."

1642   *A Paradox in the Praise of a Dunce, To Smectymnuus. Square-Caps turned into Round-Heads. The Art of Living in London.*

1644   Poem for Hollar engraving: "Royal Exchange, Interior from the West." Probably died this year or shortly after.

CHAPTER 1

Henry Peacham: A Complete Gentleman

IN 1612 in the preface to one of his books Henry Peacham at the age of thirty-four proudly declared: "By profession I am a Scholler."[1] Hence perhaps some of the attraction of Peacham, since in reading his works we become acquainted with a mind that can freely move among a multitude of subjects, be they cosmography, mathematics, history, painting, music, fishing, heraldry, ancient coins, or poetry. Indeed the Renaissance ideal of wholeness, nowhere better defined than in Peacham's *The Compleat Gentleman*, is mirrored in Peacham himself, who, never hesitant to talk about himself and wise enough, one senses, not to lack a sense of proportion, once humorously compared his talents with the various parts of St. Paul's Cathedral:

> This head of mine with sundry humors fraught,
>   To spacious Poules I haue resembled oft,
> Wherein, the Quier, for my soules saluation,
>   At morne and euen, I make my Meditation,
> My Musicke takes another place, hard by,
>   Next painting, guilding and my Imagerie:
> Compriz'd a great deale though in narower roomes,
>   Then either th'Organes, or those stately tombes,
> Descending downe a world of *Fancies* walke,
>   Of traffique these, of warre the other talk.[2]

Thirty years or so later, however, Peacham's view of himself was more qualified when he remarked that he had "ever found multiplicity of Knowledge in many things to have beene rather an hinderance, then ever any Way-tending to advancement. Having hereby found much imployment to no purpose."[3]

The variety of Peacham's many activities as teacher, painter, writer, social critic, antiquarian, self-appointed war correspondent,

15

traveller, and scholar is impressive, especially when we realize the odds against him. Being born the younger son of a clergyman of moderate means was not an auspicious beginning for one who appears to have desired above all to be allowed sufficient leisure to follow his interests wherever they took him without having to face the mundane and time-consuming activities that are often required to earn one's bread. In his essay "Of Liberty" Peacham declares: "For mine owne part I affect freedome so much, and I have found such happinesse therein, that I had rather dine at a three peny Ordinary, where I may be free and merry, then to bee a dumbe tenant for two houres at a Lords table."[4] Nevertheless, Peacham appears on many occasions to have sought a place at the tables of the great, and it is clear that his desire for artistic and scholarly freedom frequently made him that familiar spectacle of his age—an author in search of a patron. Not only could a patron offer the customary protection which most authors deemed necessary for their wares, but with luck some financial remuneration would follow.

Peacham's searches for the latter kind of benefit were fruitless if we take our testimony from his essay "Of making and publishing Bookes" in which he claims that "I never gained one halfe-penny by any Dedication that ever I made, save *splendida promissa.*"[5] His experience is indicative of the general difficulty for anyone in the first half of the seventeenth century who was forced or desired to live by the pen. Although at this time the gradual emergence of the professional writer was underway, it is clear that few authors were able to earn enough to live on. Nor was there anything corresponding to the modern system of royalties whereby an author could benefit financially from a book that happened to sell well. Once a manuscript had been sold to a publisher, often for quite a small fee (the ten pounds that Milton got for *Paradise Lost* is one of the best-known examples), the author lost all rights to his work. As Peacham warns the would-be author: "having spent many yeeres, much money, and a great part of thy life, hoping by thy labours and honest deserving to get a respect in the world, or by thy Dedication the favour and support of some great personage for thy preferment, or a good round summe of a Stationer for thy Coppy, and it must be a choice and rare one too; (which hee for his owne gaine wil look to) it will hardly by a tenth part countervaile thy labour and charge."[6] For these various reasons Peacham appears grudgingly to have remained a schoolmaster for most of his life, teaching being in his opinion "one of the most laborious callings in the World" and one of the most thankless.[7] Late in life, possibly through the benefits of a second marriage, he gave it up: "For my part, I have done with that profession, having evermore found the world unthankfull, how industrious soever I have beene."[8] While there are occasional intervals in Peacham's life when he appears to have escaped from the burdens of a profession he hated, any fanciful envy that we may feel for his varied life and interests should be tempered by reminders of his constant frustration and the somewhat bitter tone that is sometimes to be found, as we have just seen, in his late works.

Nevertheless, whatever the odds against them, all manner of men including Peacham did write books in the seventeenth century in response to the growing demand for the printed word. Of the types of book bought by the reading public during the first four decades of the century those most in demand dealt with religion, law, medicine, education, practical knowledge, travel, contemporary news, and history. Poetry and drama, which today we think of first in connection with the seventeenth century, had a much smaller readership. Just as Peacham's interests and activities tend to be typical of his age, so too his books exemplify the variety popular in his time. For example, though for the most part rather reticent about religion, his Royalist and Anglican sympathies did find their way into print late in life when on the eve of the Civil War he participated in current religious controversy with his pamphlets *The Duty of All True Subjects* (1639), *A Dialogue Between the Crosse in Cheap* (1641), *Square-Caps Turned Into Round-Heads* (1642), and *A Paradox in the Praise of a Dunce, to Smectymnuus* (1642). Admittedly Peacham wrote nothing on law or medicine, but his *A True Relation of the Affaires of Cleve and Gulick* (1615) is typical of many contemporary eyewitness relations of recent important events. Typical of the innumerable practical treatises that jostled for a place on the booksellers' stalls is Peacham's first publication, *The Art of Drawing with the Pen and Limming in Water Colours* (1606), and its subsequent expansion in *Graphice* (1612), both of which are handbooks designed for the student of drawing and painting, offering practical advice in such matters as "Instruments necessary for drawing," and "Of the Seuerall Gummes that are vsed in grinding of water colors." More entertaining, perhaps, but equally practical is *The Art of Living in London* (1642), a brief tract supposedly based on experience and designed to offer advice of city ways to the unwary newcomer. Its practicality is matched by much moral didacticism and the resultant tone is similar to that of *The Worth of a Peny* (1641), a book of advice on how to be thrifty, and hence part of a considerable literature on what was obviously another popular topic.[9] Equally educational in its purported aims, but considerably more lengthy and ambitious in its scope, is *The Compleat Gentleman* (1622), which, in the course of outlining the ideal system of studies for a young gentleman, offers practical advice and a great deal of basic knowledge in such varied fields as music, travel, blazonry, bodily exercise, and the duty of parents with regard to their children's education. A long tradition of courtesy literature precedes it, and, given its comprehensive attractions, this was, not surprisingly, the most popular of Peacham's books during his lifetime.

In addition to these works are Peacham's more literary compositions: his emblem book *Minerva Britanna* (1612); his various volumes of poetry; his collection of essays in *The Truth of Our Times* (1638); and his collection of "rarities" translated from other writers in *The Valley of Varietie* (1638).

I *Early Life and Education*

Henry Peacham was born in 1578 in North Mymms (Hertfordshire), the birthplace, he was fond of reminding readers, of Thomas More and John Heywood (the epigrammatist). His father, also named Henry, was a clergyman and is remembered today as the author of one of the most important English rhetorical treatises, *The Garden of Eloquence* (1577). A man of wide reading, particularly in the classics, the elder Henry Peacham sent his son to school locally and later to a school in London.[10] In the classroom the boy's talents in drawing quickly showed themselves but were not appreciated, something that Peacham later remembered when he wrote *The Art of Drawing*, somewhat defiantly one feels, "for the benefit of many young Gentlemen, who were my Schollers for the Latine and Greek tongues."[11] As he wrote this work, and as he taught his own students to draw,[12] he must frequently have been reminded of his own experiences at school, one of which he relates in *The Compleat Gentleman:*

Painting is a quality I loue (I confesse) and admire in others, because euer naturally from a child, I haue beene addicted to the practise hereof; yet when I was young, I haue beene cruelly beaten by ill and ignorant schoolemasters, when I haue beene taking, in white and blacke, the countenance of some one or other (which I could do at thirteene and four-teene yeares of age) [. . .] yet could they neuer beate it out of me. I remember one Master I had (and yet liuing not farre from *S. Albanes*) took me one time drawing out with my pen that peare-tree and boyes throwing at it, at the end of the Latine Grammar: which he perceiuing, in a rage strooke mee with the great end of the rodde, and rent my paper, swearing it was the onely way to teach mee to robbe Orchards; beside, that I was placed with him to bee made a scholler and not a painter, which I was very likely to doe.[13]

In 1592, at the age of fourteen, Peacham matriculated at Trinity College, Cambridge as a sizar, one who performed various menial tasks about the college in return for assistance toward fees. When he arrived at Cambridge, Trinity College, as we know from Hamond's map of the city (1592), was as yet without its now famous Great Court, and meadowlands covered the site where the magnificent quadrangle known as Nevile's Court now stands. Even so, for the lowly fourteen-year-old sizar, Trinity must indeed have been a "princely house" (to quote Roger Ascham's description), both for its physical facilities and for the intellectual stimulus to be derived from joining its scholarly community of Master, senior fellows, and students. In *Minerva Britanna* Peacham refers to "Cambridge and heerin Trinitie Colledge" as "my ever-loved Mother,/ From whome this little that I haue I drew,"[14] and, once he began to publish books, he tended to sign their title pages with proud reminders of his having been "Sometimes of Trinity Colledge Cambridge." Not least among his later tributes to Cambridge were his praise of "that noble and worthy-minded gentleman Mr. Dr. Nevil our Master of Trinitie Colledge" and the emblem in *Minerva Britanna* addressed to his tutor John Layfield,[15] who was lector linguae Graecae in 1593 and was apparently "skilled in architecture."[16] Peacham graduated B.A. in 1595 and M.A. three years later.

II *Early Drawings*

Whether it was Layfield's interest in architecture that encouraged Peacham to continue drawing, one does not know, but Peacham tells us that at Cambridge he drew a "mappe" of the town "accord-ing to Geometricall proportion,"[17] something akin perhaps to the kind of two-dimensional perspective views of cities that many an

engraver of the time produced. Peacham's "mappe" has not survived, but another early drawing has. The year he completed his
B.A. he was responsible for what is today one of the most important
and familiar surviving pieces of visual evidence regarding the
Elizabethan theater—the first known illustration of a Shakespearean
play in performance; a scene from *Titus Andronicus*. In the drawing
Tamora and two sons are shown kneeling before Titus. Aaron, the
Moor, stands with bared sword behind them. Beneath are written
lines from Acts I and V, though these do not precisely match any
extant version of the original printed texts, thereby posing something of a puzzle for textual scholars.[18] The drawing also has particular interest for scholars because of its indication of the apparently anachronistic methods of costuming Roman plays in the
Elizabethan theater, and because of the very dark coloration of
Aaron, a matter of special concern in debates about how Othello was
presented. The drawing is signed "Henricus Peacham Anno m° q° g
qᵗᵒ (i.e., 1595 or possibly 1594). Moreover, the document is en-
dorsed "Henrye Peachams Hande 1595" in an Elizabethan script,
but this may be a fabrication by the forger John Payne Collier.[19]

III *Early Travels and First Teaching Post*

Precisely what Peacham did after completing his B.A. is not clear.
Officially, Cambridge still required three years of resident study for
the M.A., but frequent dispensations were awarded.[20] Peacham
may have gone to Lincolnshire where his father was granted the
living of South Leverton on 21 March, 1595. Certainly the younger
Henry was in Leverton in 1597, though perhaps only during a vacation, for while he was there, he carved his name and age on an
interior stone window ledge of his father's church, St. Helena's:
"HENRY PECHAM: AEᵗ 19 1597."[21]

At about this time the young Henry Peacham must also have
begun his travels in England in search of anything of antiquarian
interest. Like such men of his age as Robert Cotton, John Selden,
and William Camden, Peacham was fascinated by the relics of the
past, many of which had either been deliberately ruined or destroyed at the Reformation or had been allowed to fall into decay
through negligence. Throughout his works he never misses an opportunity of telling his readers about what he has seen in his travels.
In *The Art of Drawing*, for example, after lauding the merits of the
stained glass in King's College Chapel, Cambridge, and in Henry

VII's Chapel in Westminster Abbey, he refers to the "many good peeces els in diuers other places, as Canterbury, Lincolne, &c: vnto which being drawne by their own antiquitye, and loue of arte, I haue in a manner gone in pilgrimage, neither, as I thought loosing my labour, since I can shew almost 8 hundred seuerall auncient coates, which out of old and decaied windowes, I haue entertained from the iniury of rude hands, and fowle weather."[22]

Shortly after completing his studies at Cambridge, Peacham may have gone to Italy. In his chapter on music in *The Compleat Gentleman* he refers to "mine owne Master, *Horatio Vecchi* of *Modena*."[23] Vecchi was a noted composer, poet, and teacher at the Court of Modena between 1595 and 1604, dying early in 1605; perhaps Peacham was talking only metaphorically, for he gives us no characteristic personal anecdotes of Vecchi. Whatever the case, it is clear that by the early 1600s Peacham was faced with the problem of producing a livelihood for himself. Nearly forty years later he recalled this moment. Quoting the twenty-seventh Psalm he declared: "*When my Father and Mother forsooke me, thou oh Lord tookest me up:* which freely I confesse, I may say my selfe, being left young to the wide world to seek my fortune."[24] Peacham's decision was to turn to teaching, that traditional standby of the needy scholar, and his first post was at the free grammar school (founded in 1600) in the town of Kimbolton in Huntingdonshire.[25] It was here that he began to write.

IV   *Early Emblem Books and Publications*

The first sign of Peacham's literary activities appeared when the new King James journeyed south in 1603 from Edinburgh to London and stayed with Sir Oliver Cromwell in Huntingdon only eight miles from Kimbolton. There Peacham, so he tells us, presented James with one or two of his emblems,[26] and as part of the lavish celebrations at Cromwell's house, Hinchingbrooke Priory, there may have been a performance of Peacham's one extant musical composition, a four-part congratulatory song entitled "King James his quier."[27] With the encouragement of James Montagu, who as Master of Sidney Sussex College, Cambridge, was probably present with the other Cambridge Heads who welcomed James at Hinchingbrooke, Peacham conceived the idea of turning James's newly published *Basilicon Doron* into emblems.[28] Written for James's first son, Prince Henry, the *Basilicon Doron* offers paternal and kingly

advice to the prince and future ruler. Peacham selected key statements from James's work and used them as the foundation for a
series of fifty-six pen-and-ink emblems. With the obvious hope of
receiving royal patronage he dedicated this work to Prince Henry,
but, for reasons which are not clear, the manuscript, now in the
Bodleian Library, Oxford, was neither finished nor presented to the
Prince.[29]

Shortly after October, 1604, Peacham completed another version
of his *Basilicon Doron* project, this time dedicated to the King
himself. It contains a very obvious plea for patronage since Peacham
complains about the difficulty of composing his emblems in the
atmosphere of a school, in which, he says, it is hard to find even half
an hour's leisure away from the chattering and noise of boys.[30] The
manuscript was never presented to its dedicatee, however, although
we know that Peacham eventually did present some other
emblematical version of the *Basilicon Doron* to James,[31] but this
finished copy is not now extant, and what we have in the British
Library is probably only its draft or copy.

While at Kimbolton School Peacham also produced his first publication, *The Art of Drawing* (1606), which he signed "from my studie
in Kimbalton," and which he dedicated to the scholar and antiquarian Sir Robert Cotton who lived at nearby Connington and who
possessed a renowned library. Peacham does not appear to have
known Cotton at the time, and it would not seem that he gained any
material reward from his dedication, but he did, either then or later,
gain a "worshipful friend" who shared his own interests in learning
and antiquities and of whom he was later to say: "Not onely our
Brittaine but *Europe* her selfe is obliged, for his industry, cost, and
care in collection of so many rare Manuscripts and other Monuments of venerable Antiquity, being of the same most free and
communicative, to all men of learning and quality."[32] The following
year another issue of *The Art of Drawing* was published, and
Peacham moved to London where in 1608 he published *The More
the Merrier*, a lively collection of epigrams, which he signed "from
my lodging in Fetter-Lane neere vnto Fleetstreet." Here he probably met John Dowland, one of the finest of Elizabethan composers,
who is known to have lived on the same street and whom Peacham
knew and admired. Later Peacham may have moved a mile or so
west of the City of London to the parish of St. Martin's-in-the-

Fields, Westminster,[33] where he seems to have been teaching, either in a school or in a private home.[34]

V *Peacham and Prince Henry*

Peacham was now virtually living on the doorstep of the Court at Westminster, and somehow he obtained a small footing there during the next few years. In 1610 he presented Prince Henry with a manuscript emblem book, yet another version of his *Basilicon Doron* formula, now expanded to seventy-eight emblems which are provided with water-color pictures.[35] Considering the original recipient of James's *Basilicon Doron* and the fact that the book had apparently had a considerable influence on the shaping of the Prince's life and character, and considering the Prince's especial love of "limming and painting,"[36] Peacham's gift was an apt one if he was hoping for some reward. One is consequently not surprised to find two years later a dedication to Prince Henry in *Minerva Britanna* which is signed from Richmond where the Prince had his Court and in which Peacham expresses his gratitude to Henry for his "gratious favour" and "*Princely* and *Generous* inclination" (sig. A2ʳ). Peacham's access to Court circles is further confirmed in *Graphice*, also signed from Richmond, in which he mentions having frequently drawn his majesty's portrait while the latter was "sitting at dinner or talking with some of his followers."[37] Doubtless, like many writers of the time, Peacham had quickly responded to the young Prince's love of learning and the advantages to be gained from his favor, for we know that as early as 1604 Henry "began now to be considered by men of learning, as a proper patron of their works, not only for his high rank, but likewise his relish for them."[38] Poets, artists, and scholars were attracted also by the courtly academy which Henry formed around himself at Nonsuch Palace and which, according to one observer in 1607, rivalled "the famous Vniversities here, or our Colledges in Scotland, for all sort of good learning."[39] Probably Peacham was among the "few lesse then five hundred, many of them young Gentlemen" who were eventually in the Prince's household as it was organized in 1610,[40] but his name does not appear that year in the list of 420 of the Prince's servants in the official ordinance for the establishment of his household,[41] though the list refers to several of Peacham's friends: Inigo Jones (Surveyor of the Works), Edward Wright (Keeper of the Library), and Robert Peake (painter). We also know that by 1612 Peacham was the "singuler good frend" of Adam Newton, Prince Henry's secretary,[42] and it is consequently difficult not to conclude that Peacham was a member, however insignificant, of the entourage at Nonsuch by about 1610.

That year Peacham wrote a dedicatory poem for Robert Dowland's *A Musical Banquet* and the following year he contributed one for Arthur Standish's *The Commons Complaint* together with a humorous emblem and poems for *Coryat's Crudities*, a work by Thomas Coryate, a popular figure at Henry's Court who had received special encouragement to write his book from the Prince himself. In 1612 Peacham also published his expanded version of *The Art of Drawing*, dedicated to Sir Edmund Ashfield, entitled *Graphice* in one impression and *The Gentleman's Exercise* in another. In this work he mentions "a discourse of perspectiue I will shortly publish," but there is no evidence that he ever did. Similarly he quotes some verses from a Petrarch sonnet that he says he has set to music in his "Songs of 4. and 5. parts being a subiect farre fitter then foolish and vaine loue, to which our excellent Musitians are overmuch addicted" (pp. 36 and 131–32), but there is no trace of this work either. In 1612 too *Minerva Britanna* was published. This work, which Peacham presented to Prince Henry, includes emblems dedicated to a considerable variety of people, though preponderantly (as one might expect) those influential at Court. The work is partly based on earlier material from *Basilicon Doron* but increased now to two hundred and seven emblems, many of which are new inventions unrelated to King James's book. Again with princely favor as potential stake, Peacham was also responsible that year for the portrait of Prince Henry which accompanied James Cleland's manuscript work "Le Povrtraict De Monseigneur le Prince."[43] However, any hopes for further preferment that might fall from his Prince's generous hand were suddenly shattered when the Prince died in November.

VI   *Travels in Europe*

A year or so after the dissolution of Henry's unique household, Peacham left England and travelled in Europe, principally in France, Germany, and the Low Countries, visiting ancient buildings, exploring libraries, observing educational methods, learning Dutch, making the acquaintance of well-known artists, inspecting pictures, buildings, and *objets d'art*, and conversing with any men of learning who were willing to see him. Before he left England, however, he had produced his contribution to the flood of elegies that followed the Prince's death. *The Period of Mourning. Disposed into sixe Visions. In memorie of the late Prince* (1613) was combined rather incongruously in a single volume with a second work, *Nuptiall Hymnes*, a series of four poems in honor of the marriage in 1613 of Princess Elizabeth and the Count Palatine. Eventually Peacham made his way to Utrecht where he "liued at the table of that Honourable Gentleman, Sir *John Ogle*, Lord Gouernour" of the town, to whom "resorted many great Schollers and Captaines" and who conferred "many fauours" on him.[44] Ogle came from Pinchbeck, not far from Leverton, and Peacham may have known him before he went to the Netherlands. When he met him in Utrecht, Peacham found a soldier-scholar whose "table seemed many times a little Academie."[45] The visit appears to have made a strong impression on Peacham, and the two men became long-standing friends.

While in Utrecht with Ogle, Peacham completed *Prince Henrie Revived*, a poem in honour of the birth in 1614 of Prince Henry Frederick, the son of James I's daughter Elizabeth and the Count Palatine. The couple had married in 1613 three months after the death of Elizabeth's brother and had then left England for Heidelberg. In *Prince Henrie Revived* the dedication to Princess Elizabeth speaks of Peacham's gratitude to her and her "notice of me, and my labours," and one recalls that in *Minerva Britanna* he had referred to her "By whose faire arme my Muse did first arise."[46] It was not, therefore, the loss of Prince Henry's patronage alone that had sent Peacham off to travel the highways and byways of Europe, in search of whatever new gifts fortune might have to offer. As he explains in the dedication to Elizabeth, "had the way to Heidelberge beene free from danger, during eyther Armies lying at *Rees* and *Wesel*," he would have come in person to present his latest work.

Before returning to England, Peacham became involved in military affairs and wrote an account of his experiences and observations for his news-hungry friends in England "as also for mine owne priuate recreation in the Armie."[47] On his arrival in England he published this with the title *A Most True Relation of the Affaires of Cleve and Gulick* (1615). Peacham is very vague as to whether he was actually a fighting member of the Protestant military forces in the Netherlands, but he certainly accompanied them and observed their activities at close hand. *A Most True Relation* makes clear that Peacham was with a section of Colonel Ogle's regiment that went off to serve under the command of Prince Maurice of Nassau. The Prince was in command of an army composed of various detachments which joined together on 7 September, 1614 at Schenck Sconce. After various rather unexciting exploits, the army disbanded on 2 December, and the eleven companies from Ogle's regiment returned to their base in Utrecht. Peacham signed his account "from BREDA in Brabant" but by 18 January, 1615 was back in London in time to enter his book, along with *Prince Henrie Revived*, in the Stationer's Register prior to publication.

VII   *Peacham in Norfolk and London*

After Peacham's brief experience of military life in the Low Countries, he turned again to teaching. He first took up a post at the free grammar school in Wymondham, Norfolk, a few miles south of Norwich.[48] In Norfolk Peacham made a great many friends among the local gentry, and to these he dedicated many of the epigrams in his next publication, *Thalia's Banquet* (1620). From among the more influential of these men Peacham may still have hoped to find a patron who would relieve him from teaching. His dislike of that profession had remained throughout his years in Norfolk and is the subject of Epigram 30 addressed to Wymondham itself:

> *Windham* I love thee, and I love thy soile,
> Yet ever loath'd that never ceasing toile
> Of thy faire Schoole, which whiles that it was free,
> My selfe the Maister lost my libertie.

Before he left Norfolk, Peacham met the son of the Earl of Arundel, the five-year-old William Howard. In August, 1620, the young boy had been placed in the keeping of Samuel Harsnet, the Bishop of Norwich, to be given an education. Peacham had spent some hours in study with him in Norwich,[49] and the meeting proved to be an important one because Peacham shortly after dedicated *The Compleat Gentleman* to William, and, if one may believe him, originally wrote the work for the boy's private use.[50]
    It was probably while he was in Norfolk that Peacham also met Sir Henry Hobart, Lord Chief Justice and owner of the estate of Blickling, some twelve miles north of Norwich. Hobart began building a

magnificent hall at Blickling shortly after 1616, but he died in 1625, and the building was then completed by his son. Peacham includes a laudatory allusion to Hobart in *The Compleat Gentleman*, and he may have had a part in designing the magnificent plasterwork ceiling in the Long Gallery at Blickling. The ceiling contains twenty-one devices copied from Peacham's *Minerva Britanna*. Although it cannot be precisely dated, it closely resembles the ceilings in Boston House, Brentford, of 1623,[51] and hence may well date from the period Peacham spent in Norfolk.

On his return to London, Peacham continued as a schoolmaster in St. Martin's-in-the-Fields,[52] but he then appears to have moved, since in *The Compleat Gentleman* he gave his address as Hoxton, a small village a mile or two north of the city. At this time Peacham appears once more to have been on the lookout for some form of patronage. While in Norfolk he had, so he tells us in *Thalia's Banquet*, been working on "A second volume of Emblemes, done into Latine with their pictures."[53] Presumably he is talking about a proposed second publication, and this may be the work he promised at the end of *Minerva Britanna* but which he subsequently abandoned because of the prohibitive cost.[54] More probably, however, the work he mentions in *Thalia's Banquet* is his *Emblemata Varia*, something that he never published but in about 1621–22 presented in manuscript to Sir Julius Caesar, Master of the Rolls, member of the Privy Council, and a highly influential figure in the administration of King James's government. Peacham had earlier dedicated one of the *Minerva Britanna* emblems to Caesar who, as he explains in *Emblemata Varia*, had been among the first to show admiration for his published emblem book. We do not know how Sir Julius responded to Peacham's gift, but in *The Compleat Gentleman*, after complimenting Caesar "for his sincerity, as his loue to good learning and all excellent parts," Peacham claimed himself "to bee many wayes obliged" to him.[55]

More successful, though very brief, was Peacham's encounter with Richard Sackville, Third Earl of Dorset. In 1622, while the printing of *The Compleat Gentleman* was in progress, Peacham inserted extra pages into the section on "The practise of Blazonrie," thereby disturbing the pagination and the signature references.[56] The new material that he was so anxious to get into print consists of long passages on the arms and ancestry of Richard Sackville's family, and the Constable family from whom Anne Clifford, Sackville's wife,

was lineally descended. We can assume that Peacham was either
suddenly anxious to seek the earl's patronage or had just been in
receipt of it and was consequently obliged to make a place for him in
his chapter of worthies.[57] With singular misfortune, however,
Peacham appears to have lost his new patron as quickly as he had
found him, for on 28 March, 1624, Sackville died. In the elegiac
tribute that Peacham published later that year, *An Aprill Shower*,
he said that he was more obliged to the earl than to "any other of his
rancke in the Land," and he later goes on to imply that he had been
a visitor at Knole Park, one of the Sackville houses: "What State,
what Traine, what Order, House kept hee/ At his faire KNOWLE, a
Paradise to mee/ That seemed for site, a Court for greatest
Prince, . . ."[58] Such tributes may be tinged with the conventional
hyperbole appropriate in a work dedicated to the earl's widow.
Nevertheless, to lose so bountiful a patron must have been a bitter
blow, especially as it reminded him of the earlier experience with
Prince Henry.

VIII *Peacham in Lincolnshire*

Dorset's death forced Peacham to continue schoolteaching, and
for the next ten years or so this appears to have been his fate.
Evidence has survived of two teaching posts that he held in Lincolnshire. The first was in Boston, just a few miles from the home of his
father, now an old man in his seventies.[59] While there Peacham
published no new work apart from chapters on military matters and
the art of fishing that appeared at the back of the 1627 edition of *The
Compleat Gentleman*. In Lincolnshire he seems to have caught the
attention of Frances Rich, Countess of Warwick, who asked him for
advice regarding the erection of a monument to her in Snarford
Church, Lincolnshire. Peacham accordingly drew up a model and
added "a plaine, but short and proper Inscription, leaving underneath a space for an Epitaph, there to be inserted after her death."[60]
When she died in 1634, however, Peacham's plan was not put into
effect, and posterity's opportunity for a lasting memorial in stone of
Peacham's creative skills in the visual and verbal arts never
materialized. To what degree Peacham knew the Countess is not
clear, but in the dedication preceding the elegy he published after
her death, *Thestylis Atrata* (1634), he mentions the many favors he
had received from her. The ten years between 1624 and 1634 were
thus not totally devoid of patronage, but certainly as yet there was to

be no relief from the burdens of teaching, a point made clear from
the extant evidence concerning the teaching post which Peacham
held from 1632 to 1635 at Heighington free grammar school, a few
miles southeast of the city of Lincoln.[61]

IX *Final Years in London*

Thestylis Atrata in 1634 coincided with new editions of *The Gentleman's Exercise* and *The Compleat Gentleman*. The latter contained a new chapter "Of Antiquities," apparently inspired by
Peacham's admiration for the collections of the Earl of Arundel and
others with which he was obviously familiar, a new chapter "Of
sundry Blazons, both Ancient and Moderne," and a number of additions to his chapter "Of Armory, or Blazon of Armes." The next year
Peacham probably left Heighington and returned to London where,
almost as if to make up for the previous ten fallow years, he began to
produce books at a faster rate than ever before.[62] None of them has
the scope or complexity of a *Minerva Britanna* or a *Compleat Gentleman*, but they show that Peacham, then in his late fifties and early
sixties, had lost none of his attractiveness as a writer. First to appear
after *Thestylis Atrata* was his lighthearted and amusing dialogue
Coach and Sedan (1636). Peacham claims that he wrote it in an odd
moment, "I being at this time in hand with a serious and laborious
work for the Presse, ere long to see light."[63] The "serious" work, as
already pointed out, was probably *The Truth of Our Times* which
was entered on the Stationer's Register in the summer of 1637 but
was not published until the following year. This little duodecimo
volume clearly meant a great deal to Peacham. It is perhaps the
most important of his late works and is laden with examples of
Peacham's writing style at its most felicitous. By contrast, *The Valley of Varietie* of the same year is far less interesting since it appears
to consist of little more than the reworking of passages from other
writers.

At about this time Peacham appears to have become acquainted
with the Dutch artist Wenceslaus Hollar, one of the finest engravers
of the period. Hollar had been brought over to England by the Earl
of Arundel in 1636, and one of his tasks appears to have been to
provide a pictorial record of various items in the earl's magnificent
collection of antiquities and works of art. The first such engraving
was done in 1637 on the subject of "Seleucus and Son" after a work
by Giulio Romano in the Arundel collection.[64] Peacham provided

some accompanying Latin verses, and thereby began a series of six such collaborations between the two artists which ceased only when Hollar left England in 1644, at the time of the Civil War, in order to join the earl in Antwerp. Only the first collaboration, however, was based on a work in the Arundel collection; the other five works consist of a view of Greenwich (1637), a diptych of Richard II and the Virgin Mary (1639), a broadside emblem *En Surculus Arbor* (1641), a satirical work entitled *The World Is Ruled and Governed by Opinion* (?1641), and a view of the interior of Gresham's Royal Exchange (1644).[65]

In 1639 appeared Peacham's *A Merry Discourse of Meum and Tuum*, the highly effective, comic and satiric story of twin brothers who make trouble wherever they go. At the same time Peacham also plunged into the political and religious controversy, now heralding the advent of civil war. *The Duty of All True Subjects* (1639) takes a firm but moderate Royalist view at a time when extremism was almost the norm in political and religious debate. The work affirms a faith in a hierarchical, divinely ordained political order, and the mutual dependence of king and subject. The current unrest is, Peacham argues, the responsibility of "our home-bourne Renegado's" who have placed "the Commonwealth in great hazard and danger."[66] Two years later, in a more humorous work, *A Dialogue Between the Crosse in Cheap, and Charing Crosse* (1641), he deals with religion, reserving his most effective satiric jibes for his comical sallies upon Puritan extremism, and the following year he publishes two more pamphlets and the broadside emblem *En Surculus Arbor*, his final contributions to the vast literature of contemporary political and religious polemic. *Square-Caps Turned Into Round-Heads* (1642), defends bishops against the criticisms of the Puritans, while *A Paradox in the Praise of a Dunce, to Smectymnuus* (1642), like *Square-Caps*, can be connected with the famous Smectymnuan pamphlet war and is particularly critical of the low educational standards among clergy and schoolmasters and of the unjust manner in which preferments for both professions were commonly granted.

But the works of these last two years were not all confined to the great political and religious issues of the day. In 1641 Peacham published what turned out to be one of his most popular works, *The Worth of a Peny*. After his death *The Worth of a Peny* went through eight further editions before the close of the century. The book is a lively exhortation to thrift—almost a guarantee of good sales at the time—and the same theme is also to be found in *The Art of Living in London* (1642), a short four-leaf quarto publication offering advice on how to combat the temptations and dangers of the city.

X *The Mystery of Peacham's Last Years*

The mixed nature of Peacham's last works and the slightness of some has in the past led a number of scholars to suggest that Peacham was reduced to poverty in old age and turned to hack writing as a means of subsistence. This view was ably denied by Margaret Pitman,[67] but the fact remains that we still have no clear idea of what Peacham was doing in his last years. Nor do we know precisely when he died, and we have only the testimony some twenty years or so after the event that Peacham died "some years after" the publication of *The Worth of a Peny* (1641).[68] This statement is, however, difficult to reconcile with one by William Webb of Chester in Daniel King's *The Vale-Royall of England* (1656). Webb refers to Peacham as his kinsman and speaks of him as though he were still alive.[69] Understandably the generally agreed date for Peacham's death has consequently been 1641 or 1642, but this leaves out of account his two hitherto unnoticed poems in Latin and English that accompany Hollar's 1644 etching of The Royal Exchange (Interior facing West). Their existence suggests that he may still have been alive in 1644. All we know about those late years is that he was "exercised in another Calling,"[70] but what this "calling" was is not known. The most likely speculation is that late in life he obtained some form of ecclesiastical preferment, but no records relating to this have yet been discovered.[71]

A possible answer to the riddle is offered by a marriage allegation license now in the Guildhall Library, London.[72] The document is dated 11 November, 1636, and states that "Henry Peacham of Chelsey in the County of Midd[lesex] Clarke and a widdower aged 50 yeares intendeth to marry with Anne Emmerson of the parish of St. Martins in the feilds in the County of Midd[lesex] widdow aged 60 yeares the late wife of Thomas Emerson dowager." Did Peacham give up teaching, become a clerk (i.e., a cleric), and then marry a woman of property whom he had deceived about his age, being 58 at the time, not 50?[73] Until the precise identity of Henry Peacham of Chelsea has been established, we cannot be sure.

CHAPTER 2

Peacham and the English Emblem

THE emblem was one of the most distinctive of Renaissance art forms. Composed typically of a combination of motto, picture, and short poem, it permitted a display of verbal and visual dexterity and lent itself to the concrete manifestation of that deeply-rooted Renaissance belief in the interrelation between poetry and painting: "ut pictura poesis." Although the theorists tended to argue fiercely over the minutiae of what constituted the ideal emblem, there was a measure of general agreement, reflected in the practices of the emblematists themselves, concerning certain of its characteristic features.

In most emblems a motto—usually a proverb, or some well-known heraldic phrase or literary quotation—is placed at the head of the emblem. According to some Renaissance theorists it should be in a language different from that used elsewhere in the emblem for the poem, and it should contain no more than five words. Below the motto is the picture, which in the seventeenth century tends confusingly to be called the "Emblem."[1] Pictures are of a wide variety of subjects, but are usually based on heraldic devices, the Bible, mythology, history, legend, fable, or natural phenomena, and on occasion present personifications of vices, virtues, or matters closely related to them. Below the picture is a poem, usually short and epigrammatic. For some theorists and authors the function of the poem is to provide an explanation of the picture, the meaning of which is invariably of an allegorical rather than naturalistic nature, but a number of theorists maintain that the various parts of the total composition should be interdependent: in the words of Scipione Bargagli, an Italian theorist, they are to be "so strictly united together, that being considered apart, they cannot explicate themselves distinctly the one without the other."[2] Thus, in theory at

34

least, no individual part should be merely an explanatory note upon some other more important part of the total composition.

Finally, the emblem generally has a didactic function and is used to expound some ethical or moral truth. Theorists and authors assume that this truth will be more effectively conveyed, first if it shrouds its meaning in mystery and so requires ingenuity of the reader before it can be understood, and secondly if it pleases by appealing to both sight and intelligence. Francis Bacon, for example, states in his *De Augmentis Scientiarum* that the "Embleme deduceth Conceptions Intellectuall to Images sensible, and that which is sensible, more forcibly strikes the Memory, and is more easily imprinted, than that which is Intellectuall," and Peacham himself sums the matter up when he says of the emblem: "The true vse heereof from time to time onely hath beene *Vtile dulci miscere,* to feede at once both the minde, and eie."[3]

I *The English Emblem Book*

During the sixteenth and early seventeenth centuries emblems and emblematic devices of one kind and another were ubiquitous, since they were regularly employed in tapestries, jewelry, medals, coins, household decorations, masques, pageants, monumental sculpture, costumes, and portraits. Of concern here, however, are the hundreds of printed collections of emblems by various authors. After the sudden and widespread popularity of Andrea Alciati's ninety-seven emblems in his *Emblematum Liber* (Augsberg, 1531),[4] such collections appeared in Italy, France, Germany, Spain, and the Low Countries, but in England there was no comparable flow of emblem books from the printers' presses, even though the Continental books were admired, owned, and alluded to by many Englishmen.[5] Prior to Peacham's *Minerva Britanna* (1612) there were only four printed emblem books produced by English writers. The first was Geffrey Whitney's *A Choice of Emblemes* 1586),[6] but this was printed by Christopher Plantin in Leyden and used woodcuts taken from the blocks prepared and already used by Plantin in the emblem books of such authors as Alciati, Hadrian Junius, Claude Paradin, and Sambucus. Two other English works prior to *Minerva Britanna* were translations: P.S.'s *The Heroicall Devises of M. Claudius Paradin* (1591) and Thomas Combe's version of de la Perrière's *The Theatre of Fine Devices* (publ. *ca.* 1593; 1st extant ed.

1614). Finally, there was Andrew Willet's *Sacrorum Emblematum Centuria Una* (1591–92), which, although it was the first example of an English author's conscious attempt at independence from Continental material, nonetheless consisted of "naked emblems," or emblems without pictures.[7] Considerable ambiguity is thus concealed in Francis Meres's statement in 1598 that "As the Latines haue these *Emblematists, Andrea Alciatus, Reusnerus,* and *Sambucus:* so we haue these, *Geffrey Whitney, Andrew Willet,* and *Thomas Combe.*"[8]

Such comparative sparsity of English emblem books is almost certainly owing to the state of the English book production industry. Some woodcut illustrations and even copper engravings are to be found in English books throughout the sixteenth century, but there was never anything like the numbers of highly skilled illustrators who supplied book and print sellers with material to satisfy the needs of a well-developed market on the Continent, as Peacham himself mentions when he states in *The Art of Drawing* that "scarce England can afoord vs a perfect penman or good cutter."[9] It is true that some Continental craftsmen did take up residence in England or worked there for a period. However, their presence did not substantially alleviate the shortage of English illustrated books in the early decades of the seventeenth century. English printers could of course import woodblocks and copperplates, as they regularly did type and paper, but they had to consider the extra costs involved in paying the block- or plate-maker, in having to print engravings as a separate entity, and in purchasing products from abroad which might have only a limited use. While many printers imported type ornaments and decorated initial letters that could be used again and again, emblematic illustrations were obviously a very different matter. The solution for the English emblematist was either to get his work published abroad, as Whitney did, perhaps using blocks that were already in a printer's stock, or to publish in England and omit illustrations, as Willet did. One of the remarkable achievements of Henry Peacham is that he appears to have solved this problem by preparing his own woodblocks.[10]

It is unlikely that he got much reward for what must have been an enormous labor, but he doubtless had the satisfaction of knowing in 1612 that *Minerva Britanna*, as far as the English book trade was concerned, was unique, since it was the first completely original illustrated emblem book by an English author. Consequently, it is not surprising that Peacham began his book on a note of self-con-gratulation: "I haue heere (kind Reader) sent abroad vnto thy view, this volume of *Emblemes,* whether for greatnes of the chardge, or that the Invention is not ordinarie: a Subiect very rare. For except the collections of Master *Whitney,* and the translations of some one or two else beside, I know not an *Englishman* in our age, that hath published any worke of this kind."[11]

II *Peacham and the English Emblem Book*

Peacham's talents and interests were admirably suited to the art of emblem writing. He was skilled at drawing and at writing poetry, and he possessed a wide variety of interests. In addition, he was familiar with the works of iconographers such as Piero Valeriano and Cesare Ripa; with collections of devices and impresas such as those by Paolo Giovio and Claude Paradin; with treatises on blazonry such as those by Gerard Legh, John Guillim, and his friend Augustine Vincent; with important artistic treatises such as Giovanni Lomazzo's *Trattato dell'arte de la pittura,* and Horapollo's *Hiero-glyphica;* and with the works of emblem writers such as Alciati, Whitney, Sambucus, Hadrian Junius, Reusner, and de la Perrière. Finally, he appears to have had a special affection for that most "emblematic" of poets, Edmund Spenser, who strongly influenced his poetry, and whose second stanza of *The Ruines of Time* he wittily imitated, in a poem signed "E.S." prefacing *Minerva Britanna*—an odd but telling compliment to the earlier English poet.

Peacham's interest in the emblem form continued throughout his life, first in the "one or two" emblems (now lost) which he presented to King James, later with presentation copies of his versions of James's *Basilicon Doron* and then with *Minerva Britanna,* his only printed emblem collection. On the final page of his own emblem book he promised a further collection, but he subsequently aban-doned this project due to high costs.[12] In 1620 he mentions "a second volume of Emblemes, done into Latine verse with their pictures" upon which he had been working.[13] This was never pub-lished but is probably the same as the manuscript collection entitled *Emblemata Varia* which he presented to Sir Julius Caesar in 1621–22. In addition to emblem books Peacham also composed a number of individual emblems: a comical emblem depicting the shoes of the famous traveller Thomas Coryate for *Coryat's Crudities* (1611), four heraldic emblems for *The Period of Mourning* (1613), prefatory emblems for *A True Relation* (1615) and *The Valley of Varietie* (1638), and several emblematic poems to accompany engravings by Wenceslaus Hollar. Although *Minerva Britanna* and most of his individual emblems used woodcut pictures, Peacham may also have tried his hand at engraving for the unsigned emblems in *A True Relation* and *The Valley of Varietie.*[14]

III   *Peacham's* Basilicon Doron *Manuscripts*

It was the encouragement of James Montagu, Master of Sidney Sussex College (Cambridge), that first persuaded Peacham to attempt the task of turning King James's *Basilicon Doron* into emblems. There are extant three distinct manuscript versions of Peacham's project, one in the Bodleian Library in Oxford, which may be dated 1603–04, and two in the British Library in London, which respectively may be dated *ca.* 1604–05 and 1610. The three collections have much in common as to subject-matter and artistic method, but certain distinguishing features concerning their contents, physical state, and provenance should be noted first.

(a) ΒΑΣΙΛΙΚΟΝ ΔΩΡΟΝ (Bodleian Library. MS. Rawlinson poetry 146)

This is the earliest and the shortest of the three collections. It is dedicated to Prince Henry and consists of fifty-six emblems divided into three books containing sixteen, twenty-six, and fourteen emblems respectively. The manuscript is undated but the title page refers to James as "King of England, Scotland, France, and Ireland," a title he discarded after 20 October, 1604. The manuscript must, therefore, have been composed sometime between James's accession in 1603 and 20 October the following year. The pen-and-ink pictures are set within elaborate scrollwork borders drawn in perspective, a feature not repeated in any subsequent manuscript. There are several indications that this manuscript is unfinished, and since we know from *Minerva Britanna* that the Royal manuscript was the first gift that Peacham ever presented to Prince Henry, it is clear that the Rawlinson manuscript never reached its dedicatee. One sign that the collection is incomplete is that it lacks any dedicatory epistle to the Prince, although the title page makes clear for whom the work is intended. There are other signs also. An important quotation from James's *Basilicon Doron,* for example, is unaccountably omitted (Book II, Emblem 10), and a quotation for Book II, Emblem 12, is incomplete. There are no poems for two emblems and no mottos for nine; the poem for Book III, Emblem 5, is in another hand and signed "G.B."; and the word "Finis" is crossed out at the end of Book III, Emblem 13, to allow for the addition of one more emblem. The provenance of the emblem book is obscure, but on the title page is the inscription "John Conde oweth this booke." Eventually the manuscript came into the possession of the collector and bibliophile Richard Rawlinson, who bequeathed his immense collection of over 4800 manuscripts to the Bodleian Library when he died in 1755.[15]

(b) ΒΑΣΙΛΙΚΟΝ ΔΩΡΟΝ (British Library. MS. Harleian 6855, Art. 13)

This second collection was composed shortly after the Rawlinson manuscript, and in it the number of emblems was increased to sixty-five. Again the work is divided into three books, with seventeen, thirty-six, and twelve emblems respectively. As before, the manuscript is undated. Its dedication to James refers to him as "King of Great Britain," the title he assumed on 20 October, 1604, and the considerable topical concern over the union of Scotland and England in the latter part of 1604 suggests that the manuscript probably dates from late that year when the subject was undergoing vigorous discussion in Parliament. This manuscript makes a great deal more than the Rawlinson manuscript of the theme of Anglo-Scottish unity (see below), probably as a means of earning the good will of King James for whom the topic was of deep concern. Here Peacham discards the elaborate scrollwork borders that are so striking a feature of the Rawlinson manuscript. Presumably he found them too tiresome to draw. Like the Rawlinson manuscript, the Harleian manuscript was never presented to its dedicatee, although in this instance there is evidence that Peacham eventually gave a similar work to the King, since in the dedicatory epistle of *Emblemata Varia* Peacham mentions having given James an emblematic version of *Basilicon Doron* some seventeen years before. Peacham appears to have retained the Harleian manuscript, which is probably a draft or a copy of that given to James, and used it as a reference when working on *Minerva Britanna*. On folio 36[b], for example, there is a rough draft for the dedication to Prince Henry that appears at the head of signature A2[r] in *Minerva Britanna*, and this refers to Henry as Prince of Wales and Earl of Chester, titles not conferred on him until 4 June, 1610. Similarly on folio 37[a] Peacham indulged in his favorite game of anagram writing, using the blank leaf as a scribbler for an anagram on "Henricus Walliae Princeps" ("Pare Achillis puer vne vinces") which he then used for an emblem dedicated to the Prince in *Minerva Britanna*.

From its author the manuscript passed, directly or indirectly, to Richard Munday, arms painter and Upper Warden of the Painter Stainers Company, 1639, the man whose name appears in the right margin of the title page.[16] Richard Munday's books passed on his decease to another Painter Stainer, Giles Campion, and then on to a Mr. Comyns.[17] From Comyns Peacham's manuscript could have entered the collection of Robert Harley, who bought the papers of Richard Munday in Comyns's hands.[18] Thence it would have passed to the British Museum Library (founded in 1753) after the second Countess and her daughter, the Duchess of Portland, sold the Harley collection to Parliament.[19]

(c) ΒΑΣΙΛΙΚΟΝ ΔΩΡΟΝ (British Library. MS. Royal 12A LXVI)

The Royal manuscript is longer than its predecessor, containing seventy-eight emblems, of which nineteen are in Book I, fifty-three in Book II, and sixteen in Book III. The collection is dedicated to Prince Henry and is the one Peacham gave to him in 1610, shortly after Henry was officially invested as Prince of Wales, a matter to which the manuscript refers in a number of places. The most striking feature of the work is its use for the first time of water-color pictures. Peacham seems to have been more aware than most of the symbolic properties that color possessed in his day, even though indeed his was an age when color symbolism was an intrinsic part of literary vocabulary. Peacham himself included commentaries on the symbolic significance of color in both *The Gentleman's Exercise* and *The Compleat Gentleman*, and it has been suggested that he was influenced in his use of color by Spenser, whose works are particularly rich in their use of color symbolism.[20] Peacham exploits color symbolism in all his emblem collections, and even in *Minerva Britanna*, where he is restricted to black and white pictures, he constantly refers to colors in the accompanying poems, particularly when he deals with personifications.[21] In the Royal manuscript the colors speak for themselves. Religious Faith (Book I, Emblem 5) and Constantia (Book II, Emblem 38), for example, are dressed in blue, the traditional color of truth and constancy; Ira's tunic (Book III, Emblem 15) is red, the color of vengeance and warlike spirit; and Temperance (Book II, Emblem 18) is dressed in purple, signifying the middle way since it is made by mixing two quite different colors.[22] Even in his heraldic emblems Peacham makes much of color symbolism, as can be seen, for example, in his moralization on the fleur de lys of France (Book II, Emblem 1), and his use of contrasted red and gold lions in Book II, Emblem 2.

In contrast to the two earlier *Basilicon Doron* manuscripts, the provenance of the Royal manuscript is straightforward. When Prince Henry received it in 1610, he placed it, we may assume, in the Royal Library, then housed at St. James Palace by the King as an aid to the Prince's studies. After Henry's death the Royal Library was in time removed by James to Windsor,[23] its present place in the British Library being due to George II who transferred the Royal Library to the trustees of the newly formed British Museum in 1757.

IV *The* Basilicon Doron *Collections: Organization and Methods*

The general method that Peacham employs for each emblem in the three *Basilicon Doron* manuscripts is to select first an appropriate passage from the 1603 edition of *Basilicon Doron* which he then quotes at the foot of his page. At the head of the page he adds a motto, usually in Latin, but occasionally in Greek. Below this he places a drawing and below that a four-line Latin Poem. To these he often makes additions in the form of relevant quotations from such sources as the Bible, the Church Fathers, or classical authors.

When one looks at the manuscripts, one quickly discovers that they not only draw upon a common source (King James's book), but also that of the the the total of ninety-five different emblems in the three manuscripts many are to be found in more than one manuscript while anglicized versions of sixty-two of them later appear in *Minerva Britanna*. Thirty of the emblems, such as that on the Psalms, even occur in varying forms in all three of the earlier manuscript collections and in *Minerva Britanna* as well. Other emblems are unique to one manuscript.

Another feature of the manuscripts is that each is tripartite like James's work. James gives a reason for this organization in his prefatory Epistle to Prince Henry: "I haue therfore [. . .] deuided this treatise in three partes. The first teacheth you your duty towards God as a Christian: the next your duty in your office as a king: and the third informeth you howe to behaue your selfe in indifferent things, which of them-selues are neither right nor wrong, but according as they are rightlie or wrong vsed; & yet will serue according to your behauiour therein, to augment or empaire your fame and authority at the handes of your people."[24] Thus, in Book I of each of Peacham's manuscripts one finds admonitions to love God, to have faith, and to read the Scriptures with a sanctified heart. In Book II the emblems concern such subjects as a prince's duty to teach his people by example, to avoid tyranny, to take care of the oppressed, and to keep his laws brief and comprehensible, while in Book III the emblems concern more general principles of behavior such as the need to avoid gluttony, to practice temperance, to ignore one's dreams, and to be moderate in dress.

In this way Peacham is provided with an intrinsic unity and organizational structure for his first three emblem collections and he is consequently able to avoid the haphazard variety that is so typical of such earlier emblem books as the 1531 edition of Alciati, the 1565 edition of Hadrian Junius, the 1580 collection of Théodore de Bèze, or the 1586 collection of Whitney. That the matter of form was of concern to earlier emblem writers is evident from the way in which, for example, Alciati's emblems were reordered in the 1549 edition and divided under different moral headings.[25] For similar reasons, Andrew Willet seems to divide his emblems in *Sacrorum Emblematum Centuria Una* (1591–92) into three classes roughly corresponding with Whitney's suggested division of emblem literature into Historical, Natural, and Moral emblems.[26] However, in spite of their unity, Peacham's three *Basilicon Doron* manuscripts offer no unity of method, since Peacham willingly mixes various kinds of emblematic technique. These may be divided into five broad categories—personifications, emblems of single symbolic objects, diagrammatic emblems, narrative or anecdotal emblems, and heraldic emblems—and what is about to be said of them here applies equally to the *Minerva Britanna* and, excepting the first and last categories, to the much later *Emblemata Varia.*

V   *Personifications*

The number of personifications in Peacham's manuscript collections is relatively small, but such emblems are sufficiently striking as a group to require comment here. Characteristically, each is identified by a title which replaces the function and position of the motto. Below this a picture of a human figure symbolizes some human quality (usually a vice or virtue) referred to in King James's admonition quoted at the foot of the page. Typical are the figures labelled "Philautia," "Temperantia," "Constantia," "In Gulam," and "Ira," each of which is accompanied by appropriate attributes (e.g. Philautia's mirror, the cube upon which Constantia stands, or Gula's long neck) and each consequently requiring some knowledge of the commonplaces of Renaissance iconography for its interpretation. In addition, as already pointed out, each figure in the Royal manuscript is delineated in its appropriate symbolic color. In general, the accompanying poems in the manuscripts provide relatively straightforward explanations of the pictures, and it requires little ingenuity to perceive the relevance of pictures and poems to the passages quoted from James. In many respects these are the simplest form of emblem in the manuscripts, although they share with the other kinds of emblems an intrinsic interest for the student of allegory and iconography. A brief consideration of one example will suffice.

Peacham's personification of Gluttony ("Gula") in Book III, Emblem 2, in the Harleian manuscript consists first of a grotesque drawing of a man with a long neck who holds a pie in his left hand and a spit in his right. As such it presents in visual terms James's allusion to the wish of Philoxenus that his throat might be as long as that of a crane's so that he might extend the pleasure of feeling food go down his throat. As an exemplum of gluttony the story was known in the Renaissance from Aristotle's *Nicomachean Ethics*,[27] and Alciati had already introduced it into emblem literature by presenting Gluttony as a long-necked man with a bird in each hand, while in 1593 Cesare Ripa in the first edition of his *Iconologia*, that most influential of all Renaissance handbooks of iconographic commonplaces, had noted the attribute of the long neck like a crane's ("col collo lungo, come la Grue").[28] In the poem for his emblem Alciati, like James in the passage quoted by Peacham, refers to Apicius, the legendary cook of ancient times well known in the Renaissance as author of *De Re Coquinaria* (pr. 1498) and considered by some to be himself an exemplum of gluttony. Peacham follows this idea by contributing the added detail of the spit in his figure's right hand: Peacham's witty composite here is his own contribution. As in so many of the emblems in his *Basilicon Doron* collections, he works from recognizable formulae but these he modifies to fit the very special context provided by his initial inspiration.

VI   *Emblems of Single Symbolic Objects*

Far more numerous than personifications are those emblems the illustrations for which depict a single symbolic object. Whether such emblems deal with flowers, trees, animals, or some inanimate object, they tend, apart from the addition of the poem, to resemble the "device" or "impresa," theoretically distinct from the emblem proper. According to one modern scholar, the device is "nothing else than a symbolical representation of a purpose, a wish, a line of conduct (*impresa* is what one intends to *imprendere*, i.e. to undertake) by means of a motto and a picture which reciprocally interpret each other."[29] The device is found everywhere in Renaissance life and literature and most commonly in tournaments, in the decoration of houses, palaces, and churches, in courtly costume, and among literary men as an expression of literary attitudes. Published collections of them, such as that planned by Peacham and mentioned at the conclusion of *Minerva Britanna,* were widely known in the sixteenth and seventeenth centuries, and in practice the compilers of the earlier emblem books tended not to distinguish between devices and emblems, doubtless drawing encouragement from the fact that Renaissance theories outlining the distinctions between the two forms tended to be both contradictory and confusing. Typically, for example, neither Whitney nor Peacham show any hesitation in discarding the theoretical distinctions, and indeed this is clearly deliberate policy in *Minerva Britanna,* the title page of which describes the work as "A Garden of Heroical Deuises, furnished, and adorned with *Emblemes* and *Impresa's* of sundry natures."

A good example in the *Basilicon Doron* collections of a device-like emblem of a single symbolic object is that in the Royal manuscript (Book III, Emblem 6) which Peacham composed to accompany James's advice to Prince Henry on the importance of moderation in dress. The motto is "Salomone pulchrius," and the picture portrays a white lily held in mid-air by a disembodied hand, a convention employed by Peacham to present a number of his single objects. The motto and the marginal reference to Matthew 6: 26 make clear that the symbolic significance of the lily is here to be understood in terms of the biblical injunction: "And why take ye thought for raiment? Consider the lilies of the field, how they grow; they toil not, neither do they spin: And yet I say unto you, that even Solomon in all his glory was not arrayed like one of these" (Matt. 6: 28–29). Particularly appropriate to James's statement, this is duly taken note of in the poem in the phrase "medijs quod vestit in agris." As Peacham recognizes in the poem, the lily is also, on account of its whiteness, a traditional symbol of chastity and purity. With characteristic wit Peacham in the poem places the symbolic purity of the lily against the sexual mores of the celebrated Greek courtesan Rhodopis and the association of the lily with plainness of dress against her elaborate clothes. Doubtless aware that Rhodopis means "rosy-cheeked," Peacham also achieves an implied contrast between the colors red and white, red being the symbolic color of sexual desire.[30]

Peacham has thus extended the original frame of reference provided by the quotation from James. In addition he has been able to provide motto, picture, and poem with a certain independence, while insuring that each provides a measure of necessary commentary with regard to our understanding of the emblem as a whole. Such interdependence of the parts, the achievement of which (as here) can demand a considerable dexterity on the part of the emblem writer, was considered by many contemporary theorists to be among the principal features of the ideal emblem.

VII   *Diagrammatic Emblems*

A third class of emblems that Peacham commonly uses is that in which the pictures portray the juxtaposition of several apparently disparate symbolic objects. Rosemary Freeman employs the term "diagrammatic" to denote those emblems "in which a number of different symbols are assembled together to represent a single idea . . . In themselves, seen separately, the parts of a picture are wholly incongruous but clamped together by the idea to which they all contribute, they show only that limited aspect of themselves which will not conflict with the rest."[31] Such is Peacham's pictorial representation of the wisdom of Solomon by crossed branches of a cedar and hyssop, a heart, an eye, and a book in the Royal manuscript, and his representation of "scriptura Methodus" by a sword, bandage, and medicine in the Harleian collection. Equally characteristic is his juxtapositioning of a closed book, a vertical unsheathed sword, and a serpent which encircles the blade of the sword in the Rawlinson manuscript (Book I, Emblem 3). The motto "Sapientiae

Initium" gives a hint of the central unifying idea, but one requires
the poem to understand the precise significance of each individual
object and the composite meaning that emerges from their "diagrammatic" justaposition. The sword and the snake, Peacham explains, signify the nature of Politeia, but he gives no further details.
For the full understanding of the whole one must be familiar with
some of the commonplaces of the iconography of his times. For
Peacham's contemporaries a vertical unsheathed sword was an
attribute of Justice. The serpent was an attribute of Wisdom
(specifically Worldy Wisdom), the most frequently quoted source of
this concept being Matthew 10: 16 ("be ye therefore wise as ser-
pents"[32]). The association of sword and serpent with the good ruler
was hardly new in the early seventeenth century, and Peacham had
probably seen portraits of Queen Elizabeth in which such associations appear.[33] The book, too, which Peacham's poem identifies as
the Bible, also has strong iconographic significance with regard to
English monarchs who, following the Reformation, were also heads
of the church.[34] As one modern authority on Elizabethan and Jaco-
bean iconography has pointed out, "The vision . . . of the Monarch
enthroned clasping the sword of Justice and delivering the Bible to
his people was a definitive one for both Tudors and Stuarts."[35]

At the foot of Peacham's emblem the passage from James gives
prime importance to the book, and in the illustration this is matched
by the manner in which the book is carefully made to provide a
supporting base for the sword and serpent, since "by the right
knowledge and feare of God (which is the beginning of wisedome as
Salomon saith) yee shall know all the thinges necessarie for the
discharge of your duty, both as a Christian and as a King."[36]
Peacham's picture, then, is a "diagrammatic" rendering of Politeia
and as such is typical of its kind. Not only does it assemble a group of
seemingly unrelated symbolic objects to represent a central idea,
but the emblem as a whole can only be understood, as I have tried
to suggest, in the light of the combined contents of its parts—motto,
picture, poem, and (in this instance) the passage quoted from
James's *Basilicon Doron*.

VIII *Narrative and Anecdotal Emblems*

This is a fairly large category of emblems comprising all those
dealing either with some narrative incident or with a commonplace
human activity. The former variety tend to be derived from mythol-

ogy, legend, history, or literature, while the latter are, as may be expected, often drawn from observations of everyday life and are frequently proverbial. Regardless of precise source, however, the emblems have in common the fact that they generally treat their subject matter as a moral exemplum: what matters is not the incident or activity portrayed but its moral significance and instructive potential.

Peacham's emblem of Pallas and Ulysses in the Royal manuscript is an excellent example of this category. The passage from James discusses the importance of exercising "true wisedome in discerning wisely betweixt true and false reportes." For his illustration Peacham depicts Pallas in her traditional dress of helmet and breastplate, carrying a lance and a target on which is depicted the Gorgon's head. Peacham's motto, "Quae prudentem deceant," reminds his readers that, among other qualities, Pallas personifies wisdom. Significantly, Pallas is here shown guiding Ulysses, an allusion to the *Odyssey* and an apt if subtle compliment to Peacham himself (Pallas) and his dedicatee, Prince Henry (Ulysses). The poem provides additional clarification concerning the subject of the emblem and makes specific references to speech and hearing, thereby further linking the illustration with the passage from James and its talk of being a discerning listener to others' reports. But what matters here, and in the other emblems of this type, is not so much the imaginative event depicted but the emphasis Peacham has placed on the moral to be drawn from it.

IX   *Heraldic Emblems*

The great majority of Peacham's emblems in the *Basilicon Doron* manuscripts are arranged according to the three-part division of James's book, but Peacham's heraldic emblems, which have no accompanying quotation from the king, provide one notable exception. In the Rawlinson manuscript there is a series of seven heraldic emblems at the beginning of Book II. Their common theme concerns the Anglo-Scottish unity brought about by James's accession and alluded to throughout the manuscript in the elaborate rose and thistle device employed in a number of the decorative borders.[37] The Rawlinson heraldic emblems also allude (see Book II, Emblems 4 and 5) to the fact that James, as the title page makes clear, is now officially King of Ireland and France. In the Harleian manuscript Peacham expands to eight the number of heraldic emblems at the beginning of Book II, and, as a further means of emphasizing national unity, he depicts the marshalling of the arms of Great Britain at the end of Book I, adding as a decorative device two putti who each hold the rose and thistle. The accompanying "An Epigramme vpon this union" stands out from the other poems in the collection by being not only longer than usual but also the only one in English. In addition, for the concluding selection to the entire collection, Peacham composed an emblem on the topic "Ad Angliam de foedere & unione Britannica."

Peacham's use of heraldic emblems and his stress upon the theme of union supply an important sub-theme in the three *Basilicon Doron* collections. In the Rawlinson manuscript they were doubtless designed to impress upon the Prince the enormous responsibilities that would one day be his, the very thing his father had set out to do when, not as yet knowing that he would one day be King of England, he first began to write his book and on a number of its pages expressed the hope that Henry would eventually be king of more countries than just Scotland. In the Harleian manuscript the heraldic emblems are, of course, designed to appeal to James himself and his dream for the union of England and Scotland. In the Royal manuscript the number of such emblems is, however, reduced to five, perhaps because the theme of union was no longer quite so much on people's minds, but also perhaps because this was one area in which Stuart aspirations had not been fully achieved.

A typical example of the manner in which Peacham is able to imbue the seemingly unpromising material of heraldry with wit and ingenuity is to be found in the Royal manuscript, Book II, Emblem 5. This emblem is entitled "Hibernica Respub [lica]," and its picture portrays the heraldic gold harp of Ireland. The poem refers to the disordered state of Ireland prior to James's accession and comments upon that country's subsequent peacefulness. The central conceit of the poem develops from the commonplace association in the Renaissance of both the harp and the lute with order and harmony, whether in terms of an individual's psychology or, as here, in terms of harmonious political order. Alciati employs the motif by presenting a lute in connection with the political alliance and concord that he hopes will attend a united Italy,[38] and when Peacham over a century later comments on the disturbed state of England in 1639 in *The Dvty of All Trve Svbjectes to Their King*, he incorporates a complex explication of the analogy between harmonious music and political concord (sig. *3ʳ) and goes on to draw an analogy between the ruler of a state and Orpheus with his harp: "Hard is the taske, whosoever shall undertake in these discordant times (like another ORPHEUS) the taming of so many wild Beasts as are daily bred in this vast wildernesse of the world, and to reduce them with the sweet and delicious ayre of *unitie* and *concord*, unto Civilitie and Obedience. . . . Every good Prince is another *Orpheus*, who by the well-tuned harmony of wholesome Lawes, Mercy, and his owne example, laboureth to draw unto him the whole body of the people."[39]

Peacham, then, takes what is initially only a heraldic symbol, the harp of Ireland, and ingeniously provides an apt topical comment on the relationship between England and Ireland through the addition of the quite different iconographic connotations which the harp possesses. Ireland, as the poem makes clear, once drenched in native blood on account of its civil disorder and here symbolized by the harsh and broken harmonies of the harp, has now returned to a state of order following the accession of James who is credited with tuning the harp's rebellious strings so that even Orpheus himself wonders at the ensuing sounds. The fact that Tyrone and the other rebels, who gave Elizabeth such a difficult time in the final years of her reign, had already been subdued before James reached London on his accession is, of course, tactfully ignored by Peacham.

X Minerva Britanna

The three *Basilicon Doron* manuscript collections share, as we have seen, a common structure, subject-matter, language, and methodology, but Peacham's next emblem collection, *Minerva Britanna*, differs in a number of ways from its predecessors while sharing a great deal of common material. This later work abandons the use of Latin verses in favor of English poems, each of two "*Venus and Adonis* stanzas" (six lines of iambic pentameter, rhyming ababcc) and familiar not only from Shakespeare's use of them in *Venus and Adonis* and elsewhere, but from the January eclogue in Spenser's *The Shepheardes Calender* and a number of poems in Sidney's *Arcadia*. As Peacham explains in his dedicatory epistle to Prince Henry, *Minerva Britanna* consists of a mixture of emblems drawn from the earlier collections, emblems collected from other sources, and emblems Peacham had newly composed (sig. A2ʳ⁻ᵛ). Peacham thus discards the intrinsic unity formerly provided by "the

Method" of James's book, although he does retain a general didactic
intent ("the fashioning of a vertuous minde") to provide a unifying
principle for his mixture of the old, the new, and the borrowed.
There are signs, too, that Peacham has attempted to impose some
suitable shape and thematic unity on his new collection. He divides
it into two halves, each of approximately one hundred emblems. At
the halfway point is a poem "The Author to his Muse" in which he
rallies his "wearie Muse" with the thought that the worst of the
journey is now over, and he returns to this idea later in the collection with the emblem "Negatur vtrumque" when he asks "What
shall we doe? now tell me gentle Muse,/ For we welnigh haue
finished our task" (p. 179). This he follows with emblems, which by
implication are related to his personal situation in 1611–12. These
emblems concern the necessity of labor "If neither art, by birth, nor
fortune blest, / With meanes to liue, or answere thy desire"; the
importance of following one vocation only; the advantages of a country life "If that thou wouldst acquaint thee with the Muse"; the
desire for a rural retreat "Such as we may neere princely
RICHMOND see"; and the importance of art as symbolized by the
birth of Pallas from the head of Jove (pp. 180, 183, 184, 185, 188).
Some pages later he has emblems on "following state . . . / Where oft
for merit, we but gaine a mock," on the entrapment of Minerva
(Pallas) by Avarice and Dissimulation, and on the neglect of learning
and the arts (pp. 196, 197, 200). His concluding poem then announces the next task for his muse that "Shall in another Booke be
told" (p. 212). This chain of allusions to the poet's muse, and to
Peacham's in particular, is part of a slender theme that provides a
degree of unity to the entire book. The theme is emphasized at the
very outset by the title and by the dedicatory poems, particularly
the final one by "E. S." which equates Peacham, "this English
Muse," with Pallas. That the task of the poet is laborious and de-
manding is implied by the emblematic device at the head of the title
page with its motto "VT ALIJS ME CONSVMO" ("As you burn I
consume myself") and its picture of two lighted candles, similar
concern with the labor of the artist being further expressed at regular intervals in the pages that follow. Throughout Part One a
number of the emblems touch on the subject of the muse, the
necessity for the rich to support the arts, and the frequent neglect of
those of virtue and ability. However, the theme of the artist's god-
like nature, his neglect by a godless society, and his need for protec-

tion is insufficiently sustained to offer an adequate equivalent for the well-defined three-part thematic division of the earlier works, and it does little to alter one's general impression that *Minerva Britanna* is a grab bag for a wide variety of completely unrelated emblems. Not until Henry Hawkins published his *Partheneia Sacra* in 1633 and Francis Quarles published his *Emblemes* in 1635 did an English emblem book exploit the aesthetic advantages and complexities to be derived from a sustained theme.

Minerva Britanna is on a grand scale, consisting of one hundred emblems in Part I, and 104 in Part II. There are further emblems on the title page, its verso, and the title page for Part II. The book is prefaced by an elaborate title page, a dedication to Prince Henry, the conventional address "To the Reader" which develops into a short treatise on the art of the emblem, the paucity of published English emblem books, and the general merits of the emblem form; a panegyric poem in Latin addressed to the Prince; and a series of poems addressed to the author and his *Minerva* in Latin, Italian, French, and English by Thomas Harding, Hannibal Ursinus, Giovanni Baptista Casella, N. M. Fortnaius, Thomas Heywood, William Segar, and E. S. Part II is preceded by an emblematic title page and a poem ("The Author to his Muse"), and ends with a lengthy poem ("The Authors Conclusion") in which Peacham presents a vision of the Empress of the Isles sitting among "The Trees of Orchard, and the Wood" upon which are hung *"Impresa's,* and *Devises* rare,/ Of all her gallant Knightes, and such/ As Actors in her Conquestes were" (p. 211). It is these devises, so Peacham tells us at the end, that will provide the subject for another book.

The pages containing the emblems tend to be densely packed. Immediately below the motto for many of the emblems Peacham has added dedications, the bulk of which are to the great and powerful, the remainder being largely to his "private friendes." In his dedication "To the Reader" he claims that there were good precedents in other emblem books for such dedications (sig. A3ᵛ).[40] On fifteen occasions Peacham also includes an anagram on the name of the dedicatee. Nine of these he proudly signs as his own invention. That for Sir Edmund Ashfield ("I fledd vnashamed") is a fine example since it directly relates to the theme of the emblem itself which is concerned with Ashfield's recent troubles that had forced him to absent himself from his friends (p. 42). Similarly the anagram on Johannes Doulandus, "Annos ludendo hausi" ("I have used up years

by playing"), harmonizes totally with the subject-matter of the remainder of the emblem (p. 74).

The woodcut pictures below Peacham's mottos, dedications, and
anagrams are supplied with elaborate borders. There are eight
different border patterns and, like the type ornaments used for head
and tail pieces on certain pages, these recur at different points
throughout the book, showing that the woodblocks for the pictures
were made quite independently of the borders themselves. Below
the pictures are the twelve-line poems, and the page is often further
filled out by quotations and annotations in the margins and below
the poems. The physical problems for Walter Dight, the printer, in
setting up such elaborate pages must have been considerable.

XI   Minerva Britanna: *Sources*

Of the 207 emblems in *Minerva Britanna* sixty-two had already
appeared in Latin versions in one or more of the *Basilicon Doron*
collections. Their original sequence is now almost completely ignored and they reappear in random order throughout the book,
often with the page reference to King James's *Basilicon Doron* retained in the margin at the bottom of the page along with Peacham's
original Latin quatrain. Occasionally the wording of the Latin poems
differs from any of the extant versions in the manuscripts, and this
may be due to Peacham's having copied them from a manuscript that
is no longer extant, or it may simply be an instance of authorial
revision prior to the finality imposed by print. The repeated illustrations also tend to vary in their details, but they are not reversed
as would normally be the case if a woodcut was copied directly from
a drawing and then printed. Presumably Peacham went to the trouble of either using an engraver's mirror or of tracing his originals and
then reversing them before copying them onto the woodblocks.[41]

In addition to the repetition of earlier material, Peacham includes
much new matter similar to other emblem collections of the period.
In the study of emblem literature it is notoriously difficult to be sure
of precise sources (as opposed to analogues) since the material of the
emblematists was so commonplace in subject-matter and occur-
rence. On occasion, however, in *Minerva Britanna,* Peacham either
names his sources or one can be reasonably certain of their
identification. Bridging both categories are a series of almost twenty
emblems that owe illustration, contents, or both to Cesare Ripa's
Iconologia which in its illustrated form had appeared in two editions

(Rome 1603, and Padua 1611) when Peacham completed *Minerva Britanna*.[42] As already mentioned, Peacham appears to have become acquainted with Ripa's book some time shortly after he completed the *Basilicon Doron* manuscript which he presented to Prince Henry in 1610. The *Iconologia* is a compendium of a vast range of material drawn from such sources as sculpture, coins, literature, painting, emblem books, and writings on natural history. Its subject-matter is presented alphabetically and, as the title page explains, it is designed as a reference work for poets, painters, sculptors, and others concerned with personifications and how these could be used to signify all manner of vices, virtues, human sentiments, and passions.[43] For each entry there is a descriptive heading, as in an encyclopedia; below this is often, though not invariably, the picture; then follows a prose exposition of the method of suggested personification which is often accompanied by references to Ripa's sources. It was to become widely used as a source-book for personifications on the Continent, and its popularity may be measured by the many editions that appeared during the seventeenth century.

Peacham's emblem on "Ragione di stato" (p. 22), dedicated appropriately to one of the Privy Council, Sir Julius Caesar, will serve as a typical example of the use Peacham made of Ripa's *Iconologia*. From Ripa Peacham took both title and illustration. This latter he modified slightly, omitting the book of the law which lies on the ground beside the right foot of Ripa's female allegorical figure and omitting the detail of the figure's left hand which rests upon a lion's head, while adding a certain amount of background landscape. Otherwise his illustration is a fairly close copy. The central female figure in breastplate and helmet, armed with a sword at her left side and clothed in a garment decorated with ears and eyes, looks to her right where she strikes off the heads of some poppies with a wand. Behind her with his head to her left stands a lion. In the margin beside his poem Peacham repeats one of the sources cited by Ripa (Livy, I. i), but adds four quotations not in Ripa, three of them from Tacitus's *Annals* and one from Xenophon's *Cyropaedia*. His poem is in three stanzas rather than the normal two. The first, in a rather awkward mixing of metaphors, refers to the "ATLAS-burden" of office that is the responsibility of whoever "sits at sterne of Common wealth, and state." For this there is no parallel in Ripa, but the remaining two stanzas which interpret the illustration are for the

most part a paraphrase of passages in the *Iconologia*. The fact that
the figure is armed, so both authors explain, signifies the strength of
her resistance to all foes. The eyes and ears depicted on her tunic
signify the received intelligence that assists in dealing with enemies.
The wand represents authority, and her cutting off the tallest
poppy-heads shows the appropriate punishment for upstarts. The
lion, according to Peacham, "warnes, no thought to harbour base,"
though here Ripa offers a somewhat different interpretation.[44] At
the end of the poem Peacham follows Ripa in his allusion to the book
as signifying "how lawes must giue his proiectes place," but oddly
the book is not in Peacham's illustration, a fact which may suggest
that he prepared the woodcut before he completed the poem.

Other clearly identifiable sources for new emblems in *Minerva
Britanna* include Paolo Giovio's *Dialogo dell'Imprese* (first published 1555), the title-page device for the 1595 and 1600 editions of
Thomas Morley's *The first Book of Ballets to Five Voices*, and Geffrey Whitney's *A Choice of Emblemes* (1586). In the first of these
examples Peacham, acknowledging Giovio as his source, uses a sim-
plified version of Giovio's picture of a rhinocerous, translates the
original Spanish motto into Latin ("Non invicta recedo"), and in the
first stanza of his poem paraphrases Giovio's remarks on the manner
in which a rhinoceros will attack an elephant and fight to the death.
In the margin Peacham translates an anecdote given by Giovio, but
ignores the fact that the impresa had been specifically designed by
Giovio for Duke Alexander, husband of Madam Margherita of Aus-
tria, and he provides his only original contribution by dedicating his
emblem *"To my Scholler Mr*. HANNIBAL BASKERVILE" and by
using his second stanza to comment upon Baskervile's current hard
circumstances and to encourage him, in accordance with the lesson
of the rhinoceros, to "sooner leaue, your bodie in the place,/ Then
back returne, vnletter'd with disgrace."[45]

Peacham's emblem dedicated "Ad D.M.L." (p. 150), a Milanese
noblewoman of fifty who married a boy of fifteen, is a humorous
comment on the union of youth and age. Peacham's poem ends
partially on the side of the lady: "Ladie, let henceforth nought dis-
ease your rest,/ For after-crops doe sometimes prooue the best."
His picture and the motto that accompanies it ironically undermine
the positive note of the poem, however, since they are joint
reminders of human mortality. The motto "Adhuc mea messis in
herba est" ("My harvest will be like that of the grass") is a grim

reminder to the dedicatee of her age, and Peacham found it along with his picture of crossed rake, scythe, and fork on the title page of Morley's *The first Book of Ballets to Five Voices.*

In the margin to Peacham's emblem "De Morte, et Cupidine" (p. 172) he acknowledges Whitney as his source, though Whitney in turn was reworking Alciati's "De Morte, & Amore" emblem.[46] Peacham's picture is quite different from that of Whitney, although both depict the figures of Death and Cupid, their arrows mistakenly exchanged, shooting at elderly lovers and young people. Whitney's much longer poem tells the story of the exchange of arrows at an inn, the "alteration straunge" which ensued, the return of the arrows, and the way in which "Some bonie dartes, in Cupiddes quiuer stay'd,/ Some goulden dartes, had Mors amongst her owne," the final lines providing a kind of moral: "Then, when wee see, vnti-melie deathe appeare:/ Or wanton age: it was this chaunce you heare." Peacham's poem leaves out the return of the arrows, omits the moral, and concludes with a plea to the powers of Death and Love not to invert the natural order in such a fashion: "Invert not Nature, oh ye Powers twaine,/ Giue CVPID'S dartes, and DEATH take thine againe."[47]

Peacham's borrowings were not always from other emblematists. In a number of the *Minerva Britanna* emblems he uses the well-known impresas of such notables as Sir Philip Sidney, the Earl of Essex, King Stephen, and Erasmus. Some of these he may have seen adorning the walls at Court and in the houses and palaces he visited,[48] and others may have been familiar from such books as William Camden's *Remaines* (1605) or the section on "certaine nota-ble deuises both militarie and amorous, collected by Samuell Daniell" at the back of Daniel's 1585 translation of Giovio.[49] Some of Peacham's other emblems may have had a more literary source. Freeman, for example, has suggested that the emblem dealing with Pallas's entrapment in a net by Avarice and a two-faced Dissimula-tion (p. 197) derives from Spenser's *Masque of Cupid.*[50] The emblem of "A Shadie Wood" (p. 182) is indebted to Spenser,[51] its seventh line ("Not peirceable, to power of any starre") being mod-elled on Spenser's "Not perceable with power of any starre."[52] Other emblems, of course, derive from the emblematist's usual stock of proverbs, fables, commonplaces, natural phenomena, and heraldry, and to these we may add some of the sources that Peacham himself acknowledges—the Greek Anthology, Horace,

Ovid's *Metamorphoses*, Pliny's *Natural History*, and Aesop's *Fables*. Some remaining emblems, however, appear to be completely Peacham's creations. These tend to occur where his picture and verse have been tailor-made to suit a dedicatee or to suit some matter of personal concern to Peacham himself. The emblems dedicated to Queen Anne, John Dowland, Christopher and Mabel Collard, and Maurice of Hesse are of this kind, while the rather contemplative composition expressing his concern for his future and that expressing his love of music belong to the latter category (pp. 179, 204).

XII   Minerva Britanna: *The Poetry*

Undoubtedly *Minerva Britanna* is the most important published English emblem book prior to that of Francis Quarles. Its woodcuts may be competent rather than distinguished, but their mere existence is a considerable tribute to Peacham and his printer, given the difficulties in England facing anyone who wished to publish an illustrated book in the early 1600s. Peacham's verses are equally competent and, for the most part, equally undistinguished, and it is perhaps not surprising that the quality of the poetry employed in emblems was not a matter for comment in England until Quarles's work, which was praised more for the merits of his verses than for any other feature. Significantly, William London in his *Catalogue of the Most Vendible Books in England* (1657) listed emblem books in his poetry section, giving Quarles and George Wither but not Peacham. Occasionally Peacham did achieve a certain poetic facility in *Minerva Britanna*. In his poem to the neglected composer, his friend John Dowland, for example, the intensity of Peacham's sympathies gives rise to some moving verses that surpass the general quality of those in the book:

> Heere Philomel, in silence sits alone,
> In depth of winter, on the bared brier,
> Whereas the Rose, had once her beautie showen;
> Which Lordes, and Ladies, did so much desire:
>   But fruitles now, in winters frost, and snow,
>   It doth despis'd, and vnregarded grow,
>
> So since (old frend,) thy yeares haue made thee white,
> And thou for others, hast consum'd thy spring,
> How few regard thee, whome thou didst delight,

And farre, and neere, came once to heare thee sing:
Ingratefull times, and worthles age of ours,
That let's vs pine, when it hath cropt our flowers.

[p.74]

XIII   Emblemata Varia *(Folger Shakespeare Library:*
MS V. b. 45)

Perhaps it is mere conventional apology, but some eight years after *Minerva Britanna* Peacham himself claimed that following its publication he had totally renounced such poetic trifles and had turned himself from such childish things to serious and useful matters.[53] However, as far as emblems are concerned, his statement is questionable, since, as he himself admits, he had at some stage during those eight years been working on "A second volume of Emblemes, done into Latine with their pictures."[54] There is no indication that Peacham ever published such a work, but in about 1621–22, shortly after writing *Thalia's Banquet,* he did present a manuscript emblem collection to Sir Julius Caesar. This is now in the Folger Shakespeare Library in Washington, D.C., and fits the description given in *Thalia's Banquet* to the extent that its verses are in Latin. In its dedication Peacham again refers to his decision after *Minerva Britanna* to give up such compositions as trite and worthless, but he goes on to explain that he decided after all to compose yet another collection because of the encouragement he had received from many good and learned men and because of his awareness of his own special talents for this particular art form. The result, although much briefer than any of Peacham's previous collections, is a quite new and independent composition of twenty pen-and-ink emblems bearing no relationship to the *Basilicon Doron* manuscripts or to *Minerva Britanna.*[55]

The emblems in *Emblemata Varia* differ in other ways also. Whereas one can detect a steady and successive increase in the number of personifications in the earlier collections, the *Emblemata Varia* has almost none. There is a similar lack of heraldic emblems, and one is surprised by the absence of elaborate marginal annotations and of quotations from other authors which had made up a kind of scholarly apparatus accompanying so many of the emblems in the *Basilicon Doron* collections and in *Minerva Britanna.* By comparison, then, the *Emblemata Varia* displays what for Peacham is unusual economy, something matched by the brevity of the work.

Where he had earlier been willing to reuse the same emblem, occasionally in all four collections, in his fifth collection, as the title page points out, all the emblems were new inventions.

All these creations for *Emblemata Varia* tend to belong to one of two related categories. The first group is concerned with single symbolic objects such as trees, plants, animals, birds, or with equally symbolic inanimate objects such as a suit of clothes or a well. In technique these emblems are similar to those of their kind in the *Basilicon Doron* collections. Typical is that depicting a laurel tree standing in a valley, the motto "Mihi vallis et silentium" expressing the poet's preference for this setting. The theme of the poet's choice of the country as the place where his muse will flourish is, of course, ubiquitous in Renaissance literature. Even more than in his lengthy poem on the same theme in *Minerva Britanna*,[56] Peacham here seems to have Horace's *Epistles* in mind, and in particular Horace's description of his farm to Quinctius. Like Horace, Peacham draws on the mountain/valley contrast and in his illustration even includes Horace's detail of the sun.[57] The laurel tree is thus a symbolic image of the poet's preference for a certain life-style conducive to the practice of his art, as well as having traditional associations with the love of poetry because of its connection with Apollo. Peacham's emblem is consequently not unlike an impresa or device for it clearly expresses (or pretends to express) a personal literary and philosophic attitude of its author.

The second group of emblems in *Emblemata Varia* is of the "diagrammatic" type, again familiar in technique from his earlier collections. Typical is that depicting Mercury's caduceus with its winged helmet and twin snakes surmounting a crown. The caduceus and the crown seem initially quite unrelated. The motto "Princeps facundus" above the illustration gives a slight indication of how we are to read the emblem, but the poem is essential to a complete understanding of the whole. As the verses make clear, the emblem is concerned with the importance of eloquence for a king and the respect it will earn him. Kingship is symbolized by the crown and eloquence by the caduceus, eloquence being the primary art associated with Mercury.

Emblemata Varia does not appear to have any organizational framework nor do the emblems seem to have any thematic relationship with one another. Nonetheless, *Emblemata Varia* provides us with twenty examples of Peacham's art which confirm his mastery of the emblem form and demonstrate that his inventive powers both as a poet and graphic artist had by no means diminished in the near ten-year period following the publication of his one printed collection, *Minerva Britanna.*[58] As Rosemary Freeman once suggested, whereas for most emblem writers the fashion for emblems "provided a casual occupation, for Peacham it was almost a profession."[59]

CHAPTER 3

Advice for Gentlemen

IN the course of his writing career Peacham published two treatises on drawing and painting: *The Art of Drawing with the Pen, and Limming in Water Colours* (1606) and *Graphice or the Most Auncient and excellent Art of Drawing and Limming* (1612), also issued that year as *The Gentleman's Exercise*, only the title page being different. The 1612 work was the expansion of *The Art of Drawing* which Peacham had promised readers of the earlier work.[1] A new impression of *The Art of Drawing* had appeared in 1607, and further editions of its 1612 expansion, employing the title *The Gentleman's Exercise*, appeared in 1634 and 1661. As the number of its editions suggests, and as William London indicated in his *Catalogue of the Most Vendible Books in England* (1657), *The Gentleman's Exercise* was one of Peacham's most widely read works, but it has been curiously neglected by modern art historians, and its importance as one of the first of a long line of English treatises on the graphic arts has not been fully acknowledged.[2]

I *Advice for Gentlemen:* The Art of Drawing

The Art of Drawing, Peacham's initial attempt at a practical handbook and his first publication, was written according to its title page "For the behoofe of all young Gentlemen, or any else that are desirous for to become practicioners in this excellent, and most ingenious Art," and (so he explained later) for the particular "benefit of many young Gentlemen, who were my Schollers for the Latine and Greek tongues."[3] The directions in his handbook are consequently "in respect of their breuitie & plainnesse, fit for the capacitie of the young learner, for whom they were first and principally intended."[4] That Peacham should have written such a treatise for his students—presumably those at Kimbolton—is at first sur-

60

prising when we recall his own schoolmasters' hostile response to his drawings, the general absence of the visual arts from grammar school curricula in the early 1600s, and the fact that there still remained strong vestiges of the medieval view that the arts were trades and were hence not suitable for gentlemen.

Although Peacham's book challenges contemporary educational and social prejudices, his ideas were hardly new; they had long been current among earlier Humanist thinkers and educators and had never been completely lost sight of during the sixteenth and early seventeenth centuries. Sir Thomas Elyot, for example, in outlining the ideal education for members of the governing classes, in his influential *The Book Named the Governor* (1531), has an entire chapter arguing "That it is commendable in a gentleman to paint and carve exactly, if nature thereto doth induce him," although he is careful to state that painting and carving are acceptable for a gentleman only in "vacant times from other more serious learning." He also points out that there have been a number of "excellent princes as well in painting as in carving,"[5] that the mastery of graphic skills has utilitarian advantages, and that the practice of the visual arts is an aid to moral virtue. Similar views appear in Book I of Castiglione's even more influential *Il Libro del Cortegiano* (Venice, 1528), translated into English by Sir Thomas Hoby as *The Book of the Courtyer* in 1561 with further English editions appearing in 1577, 1588, and 1603. In 1562 when Lord Burghley laid down a program of studies for the twelve-year-old Earl of Oxford, half an hour a day was set aside for drawing,[6] and some years later Richard Mulcaster in *The First Part of the Elementarie* (1582), a treatise concerning the education of young children, recommends that drawing should be part of the curriculum.[7] A final example of the currency of such attitudes is provided by Sir Humphrey Gilbert who proposed the setting up of what would virtually have been a new university to be known as "The Queen's Academy," an institution at which "her Maiestes Wardes, and others the youth of nobility and gentlemen" could be educated.[8] Gilbert's curriculum includes drawing, and, like Elyot, he stresses its utilitarian advantages. When Peacham encouraged his pupils at Kimbolton to cultivate the arts of drawing and painting, or when he later took his Norfolk student Edward Chamberlain out into the country to draw flowers, insects, or "A curious land-schap or a clouded sky,"[9] he was thus putting into

practice an educational principle that had been advocated in certain
circles for some time in England, although it had never been accorded regular recognition in grammar school curricula.

Peacham's treatise was not the first work of its kind in England,
even if its direct appeal to the gentleman amateur was new. Among
the handful of sixteenth-century treatises anticipating Peacham's
was Richard Haydocke's *A Tracte Containing the Artes of Curious
Paintinge Caruinge and Buildinge* (Oxford, 1598), a translation of part
of Paolo Lomazzo's *Trattato dell'arte della Pittura* (Milan, 1584).
Peacham was much indebted to Haydocke's translation as was his
famous contemporary, the miniaturist Nicholas Hilliard who sometime between 1597 and 1603 wrote at Haydocke's instigation his "A
Treatise Concerning the Arte of Limning." Hilliard's work was
never published at the time and appears to have circulated in manuscript in the early part of the seventeenth century. Possibly
Peacham had seen a copy since Books I and II of his own treatise
broadly follow the arrangement of Hilliard's subject-matter although
Peacham's work is interspersed with discussions of many additional
topics not in Hillard.[10]

Peacham begins with a dedication to Sir Robert Cotton in which
he bemoans the scarcity in England of those able to draw and paint.
Then in his epistle "To the Reader" he talks of his own natural
abilities in drawing and mentions that he has "bestowed many idle
howers in it." He hastens to add, however, that "I was neuer so
wedded vnto it, as to hold it any part of my profession, but rather
alloted it the place *inter splendidas nugas*, and those things of an
accomplement required in a Scholler or Gentleman." Like Elyot,
then, he sees the gentleman's practice of the graphic arts as only a
part of a larger scheme and he urges his scholar never to "cast off the
mistres to court the maid," since "maintaining an argument in
Philosophy or diuinity" better graces the gentleman than "intimat-
ing his skil with the pencil" (sig. A3ʳ). In defence of the gentlemanly
practice of painting and drawing, Peacham then goes on to quote
historical precedent and borrows from Castiglione the example of
the Roman Fabius, a great counsellor who could also paint.[11] The
way is thus prepared for what is to follow in the text itself.

The Art of Drawing is divided into three books. The first has
fifteen chapters, the majority of which contain step-by-step instructions on such matters as "Instruments necessary for drawing," and
"Of Drawing beasts, birds, flowers, &c." Peacham, the scholar,

cannot resist, however, opening Book I with a chapter which begins
by defining painting in a partial paraphrase of the opening of
Lomazzo's first chapter ("The Definition of Painting") and which
goes on to catalogue numerous historical precedents in favor of
according the arts of drawing and painting high status. Chapter Two
provides a list, parallel but by no means identical to that given in
Lomazzo's Preface, of the finest painters from classical times to his
own day. This is followed by a section on the high monetary value
accorded the visual arts in history, also a feature of Lomazzo's Preface, and the chapter concludes with a brief discussion of sculpture,
Peacham adding his voice to the contemporary debate on the relative merits of painting and carving by urging that the latter "is more
rude and rough in exercise, and worketh not with so fine a iudgement" (p. 8).

Chapter Three warns again about the dangers of being too dis-
tracted by drawing and painting and comments on the misuse of the
visual arts for the purposes of satirical caricature, pornography, and
representations of God that revive "the old heresie of the An-
thropomorphites who supposed God to be in the shape of an old
man, sitting vpon his throne in a white Robe, with a triple crowne
on his head" (pp. 8–9). On this last matter Peacham's views parallel
those of Haydocke who was embarrassed by Lomazzo's Roman
Catholicism and his view that art should be primarily dedicated to
religious ends.[12] The remainder of Book I is then taken up with
practical matters, in which Peacham first displays his characteristic
ability to enliven his subjects with anecdotes. Often they are personal and humorous. Immediately after a rather difficult section in
which he discusses "Generall rules for shadowing," for example, he
suddenly provides "A merry iest of two Painters" which tells how he
was called upon to sort out a quarrel between two painters in
Huntingdon and of the amusing outcome, not, as it turns out, completely irrelevant to the subject of "shadowing" (pp. 26–27). The
chapter on landscape concludes in a similar anecdotal fashion with a
warning against painting a view in the morning: "An honest yeoman
and a friend of myne was in this manner notably coesoned in buiying
a bargain of Timber by the greate in a mystie or rimie morning, (the
trees seeming bigger then they were) in a manner to his vndooing:
but I feare mee, within these few yeares the mistes will bee so
thicke, wee shall see no wood at all" (p. 31). Peacham's technique is
perhaps borrowed from his classroom experience. Like any good

teacher he knows how to judge the attention span of his auditors and how to recapture flagging concentration with a joke or a story.

The final two books of *The Art of Drawing* deal with more specialized topics and tend to be of less interest to the general reader. Book II consists of a series of recipes for making colors and sections on gilding and on "making inkes of sundry colours." Book III is on "Annealing and painting vpon glasse" and consists of two chapters. The first concerns stained glass and comments on its neglect in England. For a brief moment Peacham the antiquarian talks of his own love of it, but this vivid personal touch is not repeated in the second chapter which returns to practical matters with recipes for colors and explanations as to how to build an oven in which to anneal the glass.

II   *Advice for Gentlemen:*
Graphice *and* The Gentleman's Exercise

Peacham must have been pleased by the reception of *The Art of Drawing* since in 1612 he published a much expanded version of it. The work is so changed and enlarged, however, that the finished product must be considered as a separate work. It is on an altogether more ambitious scale since it adds a great deal of theoretical material, much of it indebted to Lomazzo, a thirty-two page iconography heavily indebted to Cesare Ripa, and a thirty-five page discourse on blazonry which includes a philosophical discussion of color. Peacham's intended readership has also expanded, and the title page for *The Gentleman's Exercise*, which is more descriptive than that for *Graphice*, states that his work is not only "for all yong Gentlemen" but is now intended for "diuers Trades-men and Artificers, as namly Painters, Ioyners, Free-masons, Cutters and Caruers, &c. for the farther gracing, beautifying, and garnishing of all their absolute and worthie peeces, either for Borders, Architecks, *or Columnes, &c.*"

Little need be said about Book I of *Graphice* which incorporates the whole of *The Art of Drawing*, omitting only the sections on women painters, sculpture, shading the human face, the tale of the two Huntingdon painters, an example of how he would do a landscape view of London, the story of his friend's error when buying timber, the chapter on stained glass, and the final two pages on colors.[13] Peacham's deletions seem designed to shave away what is not strictly relevant and to raise the level of seriousness. His additions bear out this latter point and show that he also wished to make the work more comprehensive. He adds, for example, a new section on religious art, in which he outlines his own moderate attitude by distinguishing between the idolatrous use of images in churches and those uses which are acceptable: "That pictures of these kindes may be drawne, and set vp to draw the beholder *ad Historicum vsum,* and not *ad cultum,* I hold them very lawfull and tolerable in the windowes of Churches and the priuate houses, and deseruing not to bee beaten downe with that violence and furie as they haue beene by our Puritanes in many places" (p. 12). A similar argument then follows concerning the depiction of the Cross.

Chapter Eight is a far more important addition. "Of expressing passion in the countenance" provides an equivalent to Lomazzo's chapters on "The Passions of the Minde," and "How the Bodie is Altered by the Passions of the Minde." Like Lomazzo, to whom he alludes, Peacham is exceptionally conscious of the parallels between art and literature, and he refers his readers to the poets for further examples, making special mention of Vergil, Spenser, and his own *Minerva Britanna.* In Chapter Ten, again paralleling Lomazzo, Peacham adds new material relating to the nature of light, on occasion borrowing and paraphrasing from the Italian theorist.[14] Then, as his equivalent for what took twenty-four chapters in Lomazzo, Peacham provides a new chapter (Ch. XI) on "Certaine Questions of the manifold deceptions of the sight by perspectiue" and a chapter (Ch. XVIII) "Of the Sence of seeing, and of the Eye." Further additions include sections on "The birdes that are most easie to be drawn," "How to prepare your tablet for a picture in small," and "The practise of that famous Limmer *Hippolito Donato* yet liuing in Rome" (Ch. XXV). Peacham's major addition in the latter part of the book, however, consists of a considerable expansion of the section on color, and once again one senses that he wishes to provide an equivalent to Lomazzo, who, in this instance, devotes the whole of his Book III to color and who on a number of points is echoed by Peacham.

III   Graphice, *Book II, and Ripa's* Iconologia

Lomazzo has several chapters in his second book describing the actions and gestures appropriate to the depiction of such qualities as Nobility, Mercy, Simplicity, and Patience, but Peacham ignores them as a source, even though it is clear that the entirely new Book

II of *Graphice* is intended to provide artists with information of the kind furnished by Lomazzo. Peacham's source, however, is now Cesare Ripa, and Book II of *Graphice* provides us with the first English version, hitherto unnoticed so far as I am aware, of the *Iconologia*. [15] Peacham probably became acquainted with this work, sometime between 1610 and 1612, and its influence on *Minerva Britanna* is considerable; it also informs *Graphice*.

One example will suffice to show how closely Peacham followed Ripa. In his first chapter he gives a series of descriptions of how such personified figures as Eternity, Piety, Time, and Matrimony "haue been by Antiquitie described either in Comes, Statues, or other the like Publike Monuments." Each description is given a title, but these are not arranged alphabetically as in Ripa. Otherwise the method is the same. Peacham's first entry concerns Eternity:

The most ancient picture of Eternitie, was expressed in the forme of a faire Lady, hauing three heads, signifying those three parts of time, *viz.* Time past, Present, and to come, in her left hand a Circle pointing with her right fore-finger vp to heauen, the Circle shewes she hath neither beginning nor end, and those three heads not altogether vnproper to her, for saith *Petr*[arch].

> Non haura luogo, fu, Sara, ne era
> Ma è solo in presente, et hora et hoggi
> Et sola eternita racolta, è vera. [16]

In Ripa we find the following under the entry for Eternita: "Donna con tre teste, che tenga nella sinistra mano vn cerchio, & la destra sia col dito indice alto" ["A woman with three heads holding a circle in her left hand and pointing upward with her right hand"]. Ripa then quotes the same verses from Petrarch's *Trionfi* and says: "Però le teste sono le tre parti del tempo, cioè, presente, passato, e da venire . . . Il cerchio è simbolo dell'eternità, per non hauere principio ne fine" ["On that account the heads are the three parts of time, that is to say, present, past and future . . . The circle is a symbol of eternity, through having neither beginning nor end"]. The remaining details given by Peacham are further paraphrased translations of Ripa. Here are just two of them.

1. In the Meddals of *Traian* and *Domitian*, she is figured sitting vpon a Sphere, in one hand the Sunne, in the other the Moone, by her sitting is signified her perpetuall constancie.

(Siede sotto la sfera celeste, come cosa, che sia durabile, & perpetua, nelle medaglie di Comitiano, & di Traiano si vede l'eternità, che con la destra mano tiene vn sole, & con la sinistra la luna.)
2. In another ancient Meddall I haue seene her drawne in greene, with a spear in her left hand, with her right hand reaching forth with these letters. *Clod. Sept. Alb. Aug.* (Donna giouane, & vestita di verde, [. . .] nella mano sinistra posata in terra, e con la destra sporga vn genio, cosi si vede scolpita in vna medaglia antica, con lettere, che dicono: CLOD. SEPT. ALB. AVG.)

For each of the twenty entries that follow in Peacham's chapter, the pattern is the same, and he only occasionally makes additions, his allusion to Spenser's depiction of Dissimulation being an example (p. 114). Ironically, Peacham himself appears to be practicing dissimulation, for, not only does he never acknowledge his source, but even where he gives the impression of writing directly from experience, as, for example, in passage "2" above, and when he says "I haue seene time drawne by a painter standing vpon an old ruine, winged, and with Iron teeth" (p. 111), the source is still Ripa.[17]

Peacham's ensuing chapters provide selected translations from Ripa's entries for Rivers, Nymphs, Muses, Satires, Winds, and Months, and Peacham again makes only minor additions, usually consisting of etymological explanations. Occasionally, however, he anglicizes certain details, as when, for example, he specifies garlands of "hunnisuckles, woodbine, wild roses, sweet Marioram" for the Napaeae or Nymphs of the mountains (p. 123), adds hawthorn buds, primroses, and violets to April (p. 133), and states that "December must bee expressed with a horrid and fearefull aspect, as also *Ianuary* following, cladde in Irish rugge, or course freeze, gyrt vnto him, vpon his head no Garland but three or foure nightcaps, and ouer them a Turkish Turbant, his nose redde, his mouth and beard clogd with Iseckles, at his backe a bundle of holly Iuy or Misletoe, holding in furd mittens the signe *Capricornus*" (p. 136). Although Peacham never acknowledges his debt, he seems fully aware of his role in extending Ripa's influence, and at the conclusion of his chapter on Rivers he perhaps echoes Ripa's title page: "Thus haue I broken the Ice to inuention, for the apt description and liuely representation of flouds and riuers necessary for our Painters and Poets in their pictures, poems, comedies, maskes, and the like publike shewes" (pp. 121–22). We know that by 1612 Ben Jonson and others had already made use of Ripa's book in designing masques and entertainments. A question yet to be investigated is the degree

to which Ripa became known in England to artists and writers from
Peacham's selected and abridged edition rather than from the
Iconologia itself.

IV   Graphice, *Book III: Peacham's Manual of Blazonry*

Book III of *Graphice* fulfills Peacham's promise in *The Art of
Drawing* that he will publish "a discours of Armory." No one prior to
him, apart from Sir Humphrey Gilbert in his proposal for the
Queen's Academy,[18] had included heraldry as a recommended
subject of study for gentlemen. A number of treatises on heraldry,
however, had been published in England and the third book of
Graphice follows in their footsteps, making available the basic facts
in a form appropriate to Peacham's intended readership. Later
Peacham included a chapter "Of Armorie, or Blazon of Armes" in
The Compleat Gentleman which he subsequently enlarged in the
1627 and 1634 editions. He seems to have had a special interest in
the subject, as can be seen from a number of manuscript notes in the
British Library on heraldic matters relating to the Cater family, two
of which are signed by him, though many more appear to be in his
hand.[19]

Although he continually refers the readers of *Graphice* to Gerard
Legh's *The Accedens of Armorie* (1562 etc.) and John Guillim's *A
Display of Heraldrie* (1610) and clearly derives a considerable guidance from both the contents of his "Discourse tending to the Blazon
of Armes" are more independent of sources than his remarks in
Book II. Adapting the examples of Legh's *Accedens,* Sir John
Ferne's *The Blazon of Gentrie* (1586), and Edmund Bolton's *The
Elements of Armories* (1610), Peacham presents his discourse in
dialogue form, a favorite device of earlier Renaissance Humanists,
and one which he was to employ in several later works to great
effect, the easy conversational tone and sense of immediacy that
characterize his fictional use of direct speech being the chief con-
sequent literary benefits. The dialogue in *Graphice* takes place in
the Royal Exchange where Cosmopolites greets Eudaemon (intended as Peacham himself) carrying a copy of Agostino Ramelli's *Le
diuerse et artificiose machine* (1588). The self-portrait is brief: "Ev-
daemon well met: what make you heere so solitarie all alone, Come,
you haue some point of Musicke in your head, or inuenting some
Impresa or other; this *Byrse* was neuer built to studie in" (p. 139). At
Cosmopolites's request, Eudaemon then instructs him in the prin-

ciples of Blazonry, the dialogue maintaining its fictional reality to
the end with Eudaemon hurrying off to lunch and Cosmopolites
departing to meet a Dutch merchant.

Eudaemon proves himself a good teacher, and he presents a concise and intelligible survey of a complex subject. Possibly Peacham
was wary about claiming too much expertise in a matter that many
thought best left to professional heralds. In any event, he is able to
hide behind the *persona* of Eudaemon who begins by issuing a
warning to Cosmopolites: "I am loath to thrust my sickle into
another mans corne, since it [i.e. Blazonry] is in a manner beside
my subiect (which *Plinie* wisheth a writer alwaies to beare in minde)
and which is more, it hath plentifully beene written of already
(especially of late, by that worthy and honest Gentleman Master
Guillim)" (p. 140). Nonetheless, Eudaemon covers in brief much of
the same ground as Guillim, adding from his own knowledge a
description of the arms of the principal kingdoms in Christendom
and of the effects of light on certain colors.[20] Peacham's work is thus
no mere selective paraphrase. It is especially original in the manner
in which Eudaemon (Peacham) introduces a great number of personal allusions, typical of those already described in connection with
The Art of Drawing and highly effective, providing an unmistakable
identity and vitality of their own. Clearly heraldry, like drawing,
was a subject in which Peacham felt at home and it is surely no
coincidence that when he came to write *The Compleat Gentleman*
some ten years later, its longest chapters are those dealing with
these two subjects.

V *Advice to Gentlemen:* The Compleat Gentleman *(1622)*

Shortly after the publication of *Graphice* Peacham travelled on
the Continent. On his return, he took up teaching in Norfolk where
he met William Howard, the future dedicatee of his most important
and best-known work, *The Compleat Gentleman.* While abroad,
Peacham had been made painfully aware of the poor manner in
which the English gentry were educated in comparison to their
European counterparts, and in *The Compleat Gentleman* he recounts by way of example an incident that occurred when he was
staying at the house of Monsieur de Ligny in France. A young
Englishman, on his way home from Italy and short of money, arrived and asked to be taken into service. Since he knew no French
or Latin, Peacham acted as interpreter and explained to him that

Monsieur de Ligny kept none "but such as are commended for some
good qualitie or other," whether it be horse-riding, lute-playing,
painting, or knowledge of languages. All that the Englishman could
say was "I am a Gentleman borne, and can onely attend you in your
Chamber, or waite vpon your Lord." Monsieur de Ligny's response
was predictable: "See [. . .] how your gentry of *England* are bred:
that when they are distressed, or want means in a strange Countrey,
they are brought vp neither to any qualitie to preferre them, nor
haue they so much as the Latine tongue to helpe themselues withall" (sig. Bl^r).

Peacham places the blame for the generally poor education of the
gentry upon "the remisnesse of Parents, and the negligence of Masters in their youth" (sig. B2^r) and it is this, so he claims, that led him
during a sickness to write his discourse on the education of gentlemen. Originally Peacham had not intended to publish the work,
since he had designed it "for the priuate vse of a Noble young
Gentleman my friend." This had dictated the style of the work, "the
plaine and shallow current" of which was "fitted to a young and
tender capacitie" (sig. B2^r). There may be a degree of conventional
false modesty here, but there is no reason to doubt that *The Compleat Gentleman* was originally intended for the son of the Earl of
Arundel, William Howard (born 30 November, 1614), whom
Peacham met in Norwich shortly after August, 1620.[21]

VI   The Compleat Gentleman *and Courtesy Literature*

The scope of Peacham's book is considerable, since, as he explains
to young Howard, it consists of "the first and plainest Directions
(though but as so many keies to leade you into far fairer roomes) and
the readiest Method I know for your studies in general, and to the
attaining of the most commendable qualities that are requisite in
euery Noble or Gentle-man" (sig. A4^r). Peacham is aware that many
writers have trod his path before in attempts to delineate some ideal
pattern of education and training, whether for the citizen of a perfect commonwealth, an orator, a soldier-prince, a man in public
office, or a Christian ruler. Such educational writings all belong to
that considerable sub-genre of literature generally referred to as
courtesy literature. The term "courtesy literature" is not easy to
define, but it is usually applied to that body of works that attempts
to establish a code of ethics, aesthetics, and specific information
appropriate to any specific social class, profession, or group.[22] Not

surprisingly, the contents of so-called "courtesy books" tend to vary
enormously, extending, as John E. Mason points out, "from the
correct way in which to eat dinner to the wisest and most just (or
shrewdest and most successful) method of ruling a kingdom."[23]

The tradition of courtesy literature can be traced back to Greek
and Roman writers, but Peacham's work belongs most immediately
to a large group of European works inspired by the ideals of the
Humanists who saw in education a way of inculcating virtue through
knowledge, of providing fit persons to serve the bureaucracies of
new nation states, and of training an enlightened clergy. Many are
the works of advice and instruction that sought to provide what
universities, schools, and household tutors all too often seemed not
to offer. Especially significant are the many works of advice that
either delineated the attributes of the ideal prince and the education
by which these should be attained or, recognizing the necessary
reliance of a prince upon the assistance of his court, outlined an
analogous set of ideals for the courtier whose role might be that of
diplomat, counsellor, secretary, lawyer, or soldier, though in England from Elyot to Peacham there is a surprising lack of insistence
on the importance of the military arts. The contents of works addressed to princes and their advisers all tend to overlap, and many
authors apparently saw their works as providing an ideal pattern for
a fairly broad spectrum of society. By the early part of the seventeenth century the term most often used to describe that pattern to
be emulated was "gentleman." The term conveniently possessed
more than sufficient ambiguity, for it could be applied to those of
gentle birth as well as to those who, regardless of social rank, possessed certain qualities of character and habits of mind and had
acquired sufficient distinction to raise them above their fellows.[24]
The point, of course, has special relevance to Peacham's book
which, complete with ambiguous title, was written originally for an
earl's son, but was published for and was certainly read by those of
much lower social class.[25]

VII   The Complete Gentleman: *Who Is He?*

Concern with the problem of who may be fittingly considered a
"gentleman" is partly the inspiration for Peacham's first chapter, "Of
Nobilitie in Generall." The nature and implications of gentle birth
were especially topical subjects in the sixteenth and seventeenth
centuries and a number of treatises dealing with the matter were

written or translated in English.[26] Given the decline of the old
aristocracy at the advent of the Tudor period and the manner in
which the "new men" of the age emerged, often from humble roots,
to serve in positions of power formerly limited to those of noble
lineage, and given the later much debated manner in which wealth
rather than birth or distinction was often the way to a title, it is
hardly surprising that the topic was widely discussed. Writers such
as Osorio in *A Discourse of Civill and Christian Nobilitie* (trans.
1591) and Laurence Humphrey in *The Nobles, or Of Nobilitye*
(1563) tended to admit that nobility on the one hand is innate, since
men, like animals, birds, and trees, may inherit virtues. On the
other hand, it was also accepted that some noblemen may be unworthy and that some men of humble origin could be properly advanced
by their prince if they had demonstrated appropriate public service
and qualities of character.

Thus Peacham begins by stating the familiar inherited view of the
Middle Ages that the social and political order was divinely ordained
to be hierarchical; just as fire is the purest element, the lion king of
the beasts, the eagle king of the birds, and the diamond the most
valued of stones, so there is also a similar ordering of the world of
man. At the same time Peacham maintains that "Honors and Titles
externally conferred, are but attendant vpon desert, and are but as
apparell, and the Drapery to a beautiful body" (p. 3). Blood or
lineage needs to be accompanied by actions "vsefull and beneficiall
to the Commonwealths and places where they liue" (p. 2). Peacham
also argues that nobility may be achieved, however base a man's
birth, through military valor, service to the church, the practice of
law, oratory or poetry, or the use of great wealth for the benefit of
mankind at large. Like others of his day, he appears to feel at ease
with the apparent contradiction in his twofold view of nobility, and
we are hardly surprised when any distinction between the terms
"Noble" or "Gentlemen" has disappeared by the end of his chapter.

In his second chapter ("Of the dignitie and necessity of Learning
in Princes and Nobilitie"), Peacham argues that learning is essential
to those who by virtue of their noble or gentle rank (whether inherited or earned, we assume) have positions of responsibility. It is the
familiar Humanist view that one finds in Elyot and others who
placed so much stress on the ideal of service to the state and it may
seem obvious and commonplace to us, but in Peacham's opinion it is
still not as widely accepted or practiced as it might be, since among

the gentry hostility to learning was still very common. James Cleland in his *Institution of a Young Noble Man* (1607), for example, alludes to the "False and fantastical opinion" which "prevaileth so against reason now a daies that ignorance is thought an essential marke of a noble man by many."[27] In 1622 Peacham presumably felt a similar need to battle such an opinion, so, after citing a number of historical precedents to support his point, he ends his chapter with a telling analogy to illustrate the harm caused in England by what he sees as the current lack of learning among those of noble or gentle birth: "I gladly alledge these examples, as by a publike Councell to condemne *Opinion* of Heresie, beleeuing to teach and teaching to beleeue, the vnnecessitie of Learning in Nobilitie; an error as preiudiciall to our Land, as sometime was that rotten Chest to Aethiopia, whose corrupted ayre vented after many hundreds of yeares, brought a plague not onely vpon that Country, but ouer the whole world" (p. 21).

VIII   *The Duties of Teachers, Parents, and Students*

In Chapters Three and Four Peacham discusses two matters which, judging from their frequent recurrence in his writings, were particularly dear to his heart: the respective duties of teachers and parents with regard to children's education. What he says has much in common with Elyot and other Humanists, but clearly his own experiences as a student at the hands of narrow-minded pedants influenced his views, as did his later experiences as a tutor in the houses of the gentry where he observed at first hand "fond and foolish parents" who deprived their offspring of a good education either by giving their children no education at all (p. 31),[28] or by hiring an inexperienced B.A. whom they paid no better than "a fellow who can but teach a Dogge, or reclaime an Hawke" (p. 32).[29] Like Erasmus and others, Peacham attached particular importance to parental influence, although he does not go so far as some writers who suggest that ideally education should be entirely conducted by parents within the home. His opinions must have appeared liberal in the light of what we know of the educational practice in the grammar schools where boys worked for long hours at a limited curriculum without any leisure or physical exercise. Nevertheless, Peacham's views are in harmony with those of his Humanist predecessors.[30]

A teacher, Peacham tells us, should be flexible and adapt his methods to the nature and capacities of each individual student. Correction of errors should always be accompanied by instruction, and pupils should be gently dealt with. Like Elyot, Ascham, Sardoleto, and Erasmus, Peacham deplores any form of coarse physical punishment (p. 24), and, referring to Erasmus and Vives, he commends "reciprocall and mutuall affection betweixt the Master and Scholler" (p. 24) and the refreshment of the mind with spells of leisure between periods of hard study, ideals which he himself seems to have attained in his own teaching.[31] Indeed, nowhere is this particular educational principle better expressed than in one of Peacham's epigrams in *Thalia's Banquet*. Addressed to a former student, the poem describes how in their leisure hours teacher and student would walk in the country, play their viols, sing, draw portraits or landscapes, or work on Peacham's latest emblem book, but it begins with a statement of their mutual regard for each other: "Ned, neuer looke again those daies to see,/ Thou liud'st, when thou appliedst thy booke with me,/ What true affection bare we each to either" (Ep. 70).

The application of these principles comes in Chapter Five. The author addresses William Howard who, in Peacham's imagination, is about to set out for university, having passed the *"Limbus puerum*, & those perillous pikes of Grammar rules" about which he has spoken briefly in Chapter Three. Howard is offered various precepts typical of many contemporary English manuals of advice to young men and typical of many literary versions of the same topic. Like Polonius's son, Laertes, he is urged to choose his acquaintances carefully and to stick to those of his own rank and quality, to conduct himself with moderation, to husband his time to the best use, and to observe his religious devotions. Peacham would no doubt have been saddened had he been able to foresee that Howard and his brother arrived at Cambridge in 1624 in great state, stayed during the vacation, from 25 June to 6 August, working under a tutor, but then left.[32]

IX   *A Proposed Scheme of Studies*

An important change occurs in *The Compleat Gentleman* following Chapter Five, since the remainder of the work consists of Peacham's proposed scheme of studies, ostensibly addressed to Howard, but so written as to permit the reader to assume that the second person refers to him. Peacham's earlier theoretical remarks on educational theory are thus followed by a practical proposal, an obvious and simple division which Peacham may have modelled after Roger Ascham's *Scholemaster*. [33] Peacham is not explicit about whether his curriculum should be followed at the university, and we assume that his vagueness is deliberate, since ideally what he recommends would be the basis of a good education anywhere, whether in an ancient institution of learning such as Cambridge University or Gray's Inn, or in the schoolroom of a private house such as that in which Peacham had first met Howard in Norwich.

The eleven chapters outlining the various branches of learning that Peacham feels are important form the core of his book. Peacham understandably excludes any discussion of grammar since he dealt briefly with it in Chapter Four. He also excludes anything extensive on the martial arts (his sympathies do not lie in that direction), although his chapter "Of Exercise of the Body" points out several times that horsemanship, tilting, swimming, hawking, and hunting all provide a good preparation for military command. What Peacham's book provides is a subject-by-subject survey of what a gentleman's learning should be, recording not only what should be studied, but in several instances offering introductory lessons.

X *Proposed Studies: Style and History*

Peacham begins his survey with two interrelated topics—"Of stile in speaking and writing, and of Historie." For the former he recommends an unaffected, compact style "furnished with solid matter" that is "vttered with a gracefull, cleere, and distinct pronunciation" (pp. 43, 44). His suggestions are directed toward the use of both English and Latin, but he makes a special point of stressing English since "you shall haue the greatest vse, (since you are like to liue an eminent person in your Countrey, and meane to make no profession of Schollership)" (pp. 52–53). The importance of good English to a man of affairs may seem obvious to us, but its utilitarian advantages were slow to be appreciated in the sixteenth century. Elyot, in all sincerity, had suggested that only nurses who spoke pure and elegant Latin be employed as a means of assisting a child to learn Latin before any other language. [34] Richard Mulcaster later reversed this order of priorities and wrote his *Elementarie* to show how it might be done, while Gilbert placed great hopes in the future of English oratory provided young men were given good training in English style. The normal curriculum in grammar schools throughout the land, however, remained almost totally preoccupied with a student's facility in Latin, and this was still the case in 1622.

Although the contents of Peacham's recommended list of model classical orators and historians is predictable, what is novel is his matching list of "those Authors in prose, who speake the best and purest English," and his catalogue as a whole is consequently fuller than any to be found elsewhere. The English works he recommends include More's *Richard III*, Bacon's *Henry Seventh*, John Hayward's *Henry IV*, and Daniel's *First Part of the Historie of England*.

For Peacham the study of history is thus primarily a means of acquiring a good style for speech and writing. Like most of his contemporaries, he also sees the subject as a source of *exempla* from which may be learned much that is morally beneficial, together with a great deal about geography, the origin of English law, and the ideals of princely behavior. Peacham's chapter is chiefly of interest, however, because, whereas English educational theory had hitherto tended to disregard English history, Peacham stresses its importance: "let me warne you, *ne sis peregrinus domi:* that you be not a stranger in the Historie of your owne Countrey, which is a common fault imputed to our English Trauellers in forreine Countries." Accordingly, he recommends "the glorie of our Nation," William Camden, author of *Britannia* and *Annales Rerum Anglicarum Elisabetha Regnante*, together with the works of that "rising Starre of good letters and Antiquitie," John Selden (p. 51).

Peacham's chapter concludes with some unexpected advice on books. He urges his student not to forget to read the authors' prefaces in books since these are "oft times the best peece of them," and he warns against the affectation of those who admire "well furnished Libraries, yet keepe their heads emptie of knowledge." He also discusses the physical care of books, but does not scruple to recommend the age-old scholar's vice of annotating them. His straightforward practicality, tinged with the emotional warmth of one who cares sincerely about his subject and enlivened by the humorous story of King Alphonsus who was upset when handed a dusty and coverless copy of Vitruvius, is typical of Peacham at his best. We may tire in the midst of his catalogues of learned precedents, but over the page there is always a smile, a return to earth, and a glimpse of the author's engaging personality.

XI *Cosmography, Geography, and Geometry*

The three chapters that follow Peacham's discussion of style and history are perhaps of less interest. The chapter "Of Cosmographie" (in which he also includes geography) deals with fairly predictable matters, and the bulk of it is an undisguised lesson on the celestial bodies and spheres, the ten circles that compose the circle of the earth, and appropriate definitions for various geographical terms. The subject is lauded as affording pleasure to mind and eye and is considered necessary for the study of history and poetry, and for military commanders. Peacham's view of the universe is essentially Ptolemaic and shows no apparent awareness of the new discoveries that had rendered Ptolemy largely obsolete. Chapter Eight ("Obseruations in Survey of the Earth") provides a series of remarks about the distribution of the earth's seas, land-masses, and climates, which he concludes like a good teacher with a brief bibliograpy of suggested further reading. The chapter "Of Geometrie" ends in the same fashion, but here there is no attempt to provide actual instruction. Once again, however, the subject is justified on grounds of use, since a gentleman will need it when surveying, draining, or irrigating his lands, when estimating his timber and stone, and when setting up fortifications in wartime.

XII *Poetry*

Peacham's chapter "Of Poetrie" is well known, for it has frequently been quoted as representative of English opinions and tastes regarding both classical and native poets and of the way in which earlier opinions about poetry by George Puttenham and others appear to have persisted well into the seventeenth century.[35] Much of what Peacham says is taken either from the first Book of Puttenham's *The Arte of English Poesie* (1589), which he nowhere acknowledges, or from Books III and VI of Julius Caesar Scaliger's *Poetices* (1561).[36] Such borrowing is typical of Peacham, although it is worth remembering that his age would not have censured him for it, particularly since he is merely providing his pupil with a survey of what one might call the "established view." We should not object either, but inevitably the modern reader regrets that Peacham's literary criticism is here not more obviously original.

He begins by recommending poetry as a means of sweetening "seuerer studies." Along with Sir Philip Sidney, George Puttenham, and others during the forty or so years preceding him, Peacham feels called upon to defend poetry as a heavenly gift, by alluding to its association with the gods in classical mythology and to the poetic expression of divine mysteries in the Psalms and the Song of Solomon. He points out the special affinity of poetry with good health, its power to inspire soldiers in battle, and the regard accorded it by great patrons and princes. Then, after two paragraphs paraphrased from Puttenham on the subject of past poets who have received the patronage of princes, and after posing the problem of why "poets now adaies are of no such esteeme," he quotes without acknowledgment an anecdote from the Second Book of Guazzo's *Civile Conversatione* that was evidently something of a favorite since he had employed it already in *Thalia's Banquet* and was later to use it a third time in *The Truth of Our Times:* "I answere, [. . .] with *Aretine* (being demaunded why Princes were not so liberall to Poesie, and other good Arts, as in former times) *Because their conscience telleth them, how unworthy they are of the praises giuen them by Poets; as for other Arts, they make no account of that they know not*" (p. 82).[37]

Peacham then surveys the chief Latin poets beginning with a fairly detailed appraisal of "the *King of Latine Poets,* whom Nature hath reared beyond imitation, and who aboue all other onely, deserueth the name of Poet; I meane *Virgil*" (p. 82). The length of Peacham's discussion, and the trouble he takes to provide English verse translations for the quoted passages, imply that he has the warmest appreciation of the poet, and this would certainly not be out of keeping with the opinions of his contemporaries. However, his discussion is largely a selected paraphrase of Book III, Chapters 24–26, of Scaliger. Vergil's poetry is praised for "Prudence," which Peacham interprets as knowledge and judgment, for "Efficacie" or the power of "presenting to our minds the liuely Idae's or formes of things so truly, as if wee saw them with our eyes" (p. 84), for "Sweetnesse" or the alluring power of verse that "inuites the Reader to taste euen against his will" (p. 85), and for "Varietie" or the ability to delight the reader with endless novelty. Peacham then turns the pages of his copy of Scaliger to Book VI and proceeds to give us a selected paraphrase of Scaliger's comments on a number of further major classical authors. He begins with Ovid and predictable praise "for the sweetnesse and smooth current of his stile" (p. 87) and cannot resist a brief anecdote (not in his original) concerning the discovery of Ovid's tomb, which, he assures the reader, "is yet to be seene" (p. 89).[38] Finally, after brief comments on Horace, Juvenal, Persius, Martial, and others, he takes his leave of Scaliger and speaks "Of Latine Poets of our times." Here Peacham is his own authority when he praises the works of George Buchanan, the "English-bred" Joseph of Exeter, Sir Thomas More, William Lilly, and Sir Thomas Challoner.

When he turns to the "English Poets of our owne Nation" the interest of students of English literature naturally quickens, but Peacham disappointingly returns to Puttenham and presents us with a close paraphrase of the earlier writer's views. Short allusions to Sir Thomas More and to Gower's monument, and the epithet "our *Phoenix*" to describe Sidney are virtually all the additions he makes, and his well-known chapter is thus hardly worth consideration as an original piece of criticism. Yet it does have its place in the history of English letters, since it represents what one early seventeenth-century poet and scholar-teacher defined as the great tradition of Western poetry, suitable for study and imitation by any well-educated Englishman.

XIII *Music*

After poetry, Peacham turns to the sister art of music. This was an established subject for study in schools such as Christ's Hospital, Merchant Taylors, Dulwich College, and Westminster. Moreover, music had been recommended by both Sir Nicholas Bacon and Sir Humphrey Gilbert in their respective proposals of 1561 and 1572 concerning the education of the Queen's wards; it had a small place in the arts curriculum at the universities; and Bachelor of Music degrees, while rare, were awarded in Peacham's day both at Oxford and Cambridge. His own college at Cambridge was subject to certain statutes which specified that the *lector mathematicus* teach music, and that all bachelors attend his lectures, and we also know that students wishing to enter Trinity College were supposed to be examined in grammar, letters (*litteris humanioribus*), and song, those excelling in music being given preference. The respectable status of music within the educational system was thus not really in question. Nevertheless, in spite of his immense love for music, Peacham treads carefully when defining its place among the accomplishments of a gentleman. Essentially what he says is no different from what Castiglione, Elyot, Ascham, Romei, Mulcaster, and

others had urged: music is for use in "priuate recreation at leasurable houres," and, although it is a skill "worthy the knowledge and
exercise" of the greatest Prince, "I desire not that any Noble or
Gentleman should [. . .] prooue a Master in the same, or neglect
his more weightie imployments" (pp. 98–99). The acceptance of
music as a gentlemanly accomplishment occurs in England as early
as Caxton's *Book of Curtesye* (1477), and in spite of the attacks of
those who regarded it as effeminate, a worthless distraction, and an
unacceptable form of worship, it retained its status and had a powerful body of defenders among writers, educators, and the many
gentlemen who were themselves proficient in singing or in the
playing of some instrument. Music would hence appear to need
little defense, and Peacham hardly bothers to offer any, but he does
reiterate a number of commonplaces concerning the medicinal
properties of music, its ability to dispose the mind to virtue, and its
effectiveness as a means of glorifying the Creator.

It is not for such matters, however, that Peacham's "Of Musick" is
so famous. Ever since Sir John Hawkins and Dr. Charles Burney
wrote their histories of music in the eighteenth century, Peacham's
chapter has been quoted as a source for English knowledge and
opinion concerning European composers such as Maurice (Land-
grave of Hesse), Orlando di Lasso, Luca Marenzio, Giovanni Croce,
and Orazio Vecchi. Equally important to music historians have been
Peacham's comments on English composers such as William Byrd
and Peter Phillips, and his by no means modest demand of gentleman practitioners: "I desire no more in you then to sing your part
sure, and at the first sight, withall, to play the same vpon your Violl,
or the exercise of the Lute, priuately to your selfe" (p. 100). In
saying what composers should be imitated and considered superior,
Peacham is without question giving a personal opinion, for in this
instance (apart perhaps from Thomas Morley, author of *A Plaine and
Easie Introduction to Practicall Music*, there is no musical Puttenham or Scaliger standing at his shoulder. At the same time
Peacham's comments tend to be more specific than those on poetry
in the preceding chapter—those on Vergil were something of an
exception—and he is quite capable of being fairly technical as when
he points out with regard to Luca Marenzio that "sometime an
ouer-sight (which might be the Printers fault) of two *eights*, or *fifts*
escape him; as between the *Tenor* and *Base* in the last close, of, *I
must depart all haplesse*: ending according to the nature of the
Dittie most artificially, with a Minim rest" (p. 101).[39] Sadly,

Peacham's discussion of individual composers terminates abruptly
in order, so he says, "to auoide tediousnesse" (p. 103), the chapter
concluding with five paragraphs in praise of music, the tone of which
leaves us in no doubt as to the special affection he had for this art.

XIV *Painting and Drawing*

Peacham's views on the place of drawing and painting in education have already been discussed, and nothing more needs to be
added here, especially as the first part of Peacham's chapter "Of
Drawing, Limming, and Painting" provides, in a highly condensed
form, a survey of much of the material already to be found in his
earlier treatises on the subject. Indeed, he recommends at one
point that his reader purchase *The Gentleman's Exercise* where he
will find more detailed instructions for "whatsoeuer is needfull to be
knowne of a practitioner" (pp. 99–100). There are some additions,
however: he praises the skill of his countryman Nathaniel Bacon and
tells the story of his own punishment when sketching in the back of
Lily's grammar (p. 107).[40]
Peacham also introduces a completely new topic. For sixteen
pages he provides a series of lives of Italian painters, and, as he was
the first to translate Ripa in Book II of *Graphice*, so here he provides
the earliest English translation of another influential Italian work,
Vasari's *Le vite de'piu eccellenti architetti, pittori et scultori italiani*.[41]
Vasari had published the first edition of his work in 1550, and in
1568 a new expanded edition appeared. According to Peacham, the
work was hard to come by in England (p. 137) and, while his friends
"M. Doctor Mountford late Prebend of Pauls" and Inigo Jones each
owned copies, he himself had not been able to consult one. However, he had seen the translation of Carel van Mander in Dutch, and
it was this he used for his own selected translation of eighteen of
Vasari's lives. [42] Peacham's motive is presumably to provide readers
who did not know Italian with a condensed version of a work that
today is still an important source for the history of Italian Renaissance art. At the same time he is in effect adding yet another lesson
to the great variety that make up this book, he himself changing
roles in mid-chapter from drawing master to art historian.

XV *Blazonry*

In "Of Armorie and Blazonrie" Peacham again takes up a concern in *Graphice*. As in the earlier work, he recognizes that heraldry
is a means of providing nobility with "outward ensignes and badges

of Vertue," and he urges its study, since "for a Gentleman Honor-
ably descended, to be utterly ignorant herein, argueth in him either
a disregard of his owne worth, a weaknesse of concept, or indisposi-
tion to Armes and Honorable Action; sometime mere Ideotisme"
(pp. 138, 139). He then proceeds with a lengthy lesson on blazonry.
Many of the technical details that he gave in *Graphice* are here
omitted, but in their place he expands his earlier discussions of the
office of a herald and of shields, and adds a number of new sections
containing descriptive examples of the history of heraldry. Most
notable, however, is a long twenty-seven-page section entitled "The
practise of Blazonrie." This imitates the pattern employed by Guillim in *A Display of Heraldrie* by presenting a variety of woodcut
illustrations of shields which he then analyzes according to the principles of blazonry. Eight of his thirty examples are borrowed directly from Guillim,[43] but Peacham usually adds additional material
on the family history and genealogy of the owner of each shield.

Viewed within the total framework of *The Compleat Gentleman* ,
the forty-five-page chapter "Of Armorie and Blazonrie," like the
twenty-nine pages on drawing, disturbs the general balance of the
book, since Peacham permits himself an element of self-indulgence
by discussing at length a topic in which he is interested and particularly well versed but which does not deserve such relative prominence. By comparison, "Of Stile and Historie" was only allowed
fifteen pages, "Of Cosmography" nine, and "Of Geometrie" six.

XVI   *Bodily Exercise*

Earlier in his book Peacham had discussed three important leisure activities: poetry, music, and drawing. His chapter on physical
exercise ("Of Exercise of the Body") adds a fourth. Horsemanship,
tilting, hawking, and hunting had always been considered important
and appropriate activities for a noble or gentleman, necessary to
prepare him for war and to provide him with suitable outdoor leisure. The Humanists had stressed the importance of physical training for the scholar whose body in medieval times had been sadly
neglected, and in this matter, as so often, Peacham is in agreement.
At the beginning of his chapter, he conducts his student from his
"priuate studie and contemplation" and brings him "abroad into the
open fields" (p. 177) where he recommends horsemanship, running,
leaping, swimming, archery, hunting, and hawking as aids to mental
vigor, to preparation for command and service to the state in time of

war, and to general good health. Not unexpectedly Peacham coun-
sels moderation and speaks disapprovingly of those that enjoy outdoor leisure activities so much "that they neuer care for keeping
within" (p. 184). Somewhat surprisingly he never mentions the in-
door exercise of dancing to which Elyot, Ascham, Mulcaster, Gilbert, and Cleland had all given their approval, but perhaps
Peacham's pronounced tendency to misogyny took precedence over
his love of music, and he felt the topic was best ignored.[44]

XVII   *Reputation*

One of the most common assertions in all courtesy literature is the
Platonic view that the man of authority must first be a good man. Sir
Thomas Elyot had characteristically devoted two-thirds of *The Governor* to requisite virtues, and those English authors who followed
him with treatises on the nobility and on gentlemanly conduct were
hardly less restrained in this matter, often creating elaborate
schemes of ideal moral behavior which they gathered largely from
Aristotle and Plato. Justice, Faith, Fortitude, Patience, Magnanim-
ity, Liberality, Sapience, and Temperance are among those virtues
most frequently found in such schemes, and Peacham's chapter
begins on a familiar note with a discussion of "*Temperance* and that
Moderation of the minde, wherewith as a bridle wee curbe and
breake our ranke and vnruly Passions" (p. 185). However, Peacham
is principally concerned with how a gentleman establishes and retains a reputation in the eyes of others, and consequently his chapter tends only to be concerned with manners and external signs of
virtue. This is not to say that he forgets that manners should properly derive from an expression of a moral point of view, as is clear
from the way in which he talks of the role of piety (p. 186). But he
reminds his student that learning should be used in the service of
both oneself and others; he suggests a careful choice of friends and
advisers and an avoidance of overfamiliarity with those of lower
rank; he makes the traditional distinction between prodigality and
liberality; and he speaks in favor of modest apparel, a moderate diet,
and free and affable discourse at mealtime, even recommending
various forms of witty verbal conceits appropriate to the entertainment of guests. The chapter makes no attempt to offer the all-inclu-
sive guide to moral behavior that one finds in Elyot, and in this
respect it is perhaps closer to Ascham's brief survey of manners in
The Scholemaster.

XVIII   *Travel*

The final chapter of the 1622 edition of *The Compleat Gentleman*
is concerned with travel. Unlike some of his predecessors and contemporaries,[45] Peacham recommends with considerable warmth the
taking of a foreign tour. The tour as a key feature of the gentleman's
education was well established in Peacham's day, and by the early
seventeenth century, as Lawrence Stone has pointed out, "Five
overlapping cultural ideals, those of the man of war, the man of
learning, the statesman, the polished cavalier, and the virtuoso all
demanded educational training abroad, and thus contrived to
stimulate a remarkable growth of foreign travel among the English
nobility and gentry."[46] Peacham himself appears to have benefitted
much from his own travels in France, the Low Countries, Germany,
and perhaps Italy. In this chapter he outlines the manner in which
travel has been recommended by previous authorities and suggests
how it helps one to appreciate one's own country, to understand
foreign affairs, and to broaden experience. Peacham warns of the
dangers of physical sickness and of corruption of the mind, particularly, he implies, by contact abroad with Roman Catholicism. There
is a fairly detailed lesson on French and Spanish customs, manners,
and architecture, and for information about Italy, Germany, and
other countries he recommends George Sandy's *Relation of a Journey Began* 1610 (1615), his book ending without flourish as Peacham
wishes his reader "all happinesse to your selfe, and prosperous suc-
cesse to your studies" (p.211).

The education of Peacham's student is thus complete, although
Peacham is very conscious that his book is "but as so many keies to
leade you into far fairer roomes." This is certainly true, but we can
also perceive that, while it provides a wonderful compendium of the
traditional Humanist ideals derived from Italian Renaissance writers, Erasmus, Vives, and the English educators such as Elyot, it
nevertheless is curiously unbalanced in terms of the special attention it pays to certain subjects that we know were of great personal
interest to Peacham. We happily forgive him for this since it is the
chapters on drawing, music, and heraldry that are the most original,
but it is well to remind ourselves that, however "representative"
Peacham may appear to be in terms of his Humanist point of view,
he does have pronounced biases of which the reader should be
aware.

XIX   *The Second Edition of* The Compleat Gentleman:
A Bibliographical Problem

All copies of the second edition of *The Compleat Gentleman*
which I have been able to see possess printed title pages stating that
the book was "Printed for FRANCIS CONSTABLE, and are to be
sold at his shop in Pauls Church-yard, at the Signe of the Crane.
1627." However, such copies often contain the 1622 engraved title
page in altered form to bear one of several dates and addresses. To
confuse matters, the *Catalogue of the Printed Books Preserved at
Haigh Hall, Wigan*, contains a description of a copy with what appears to be a version of the 1622 engraved title page, now altered to
include the words "The second Impression much Inlarged anno
1626. Imprinted at London for Francis Constable and are to bee
sold at his shoppe in pauls Church yeard at ye crane. 1626," but the
collation of this text matches that of the 1622 edition, and the book
would therefore appear to be a reissue of the first edition with an
altered title page.[47] Further variations are represented first by a
Folger Shakespeare Library copy which has a 1627 text accompanied by an engraved title page on which Constable's address is
given as "ye Greene man in Leaden hall street right over Billeter
lane," the engraving being dated 1625, and second by a copy once
described by Hazlitt as "The second Impression, much Inlarged.
Anno 1626. Imprinted at London for Francis Constable, &c. Title
engraved by Delarum."[48] What is notable about this copy is that it
apparently contained the arms of George Villiers, Duke of Buckingham,[49] and a dedication to him (neither of which appear in any copy
I have examined), together with the dedication to William Howard.
The collation of the text which Hazlitt provides matches that of the
1627 copies (A-2H^2 in fours), but the preliminary matter in gather-
ing A is different in content and arrangement except for the dedication to Howard. The title page described by Hazitt appears, from
what little information he gives, to be identical with the engraved
title page of the British Library copy of the 1627 text (C. 175. ff21)
which has the words "The second Impression much Inlarged Anno
1626. Imprinted at London for Francis Constable and are to bee
sold at his shoope in pauls Church yeard at ye crane. Fr Delarum
Sculp. Anno 1626."

It would thus appear that in 1626 there may have been a reissue of
the 1622 edition with an altered engraved title page dated appro-

priately. Versions of the engraved title page dated 1625, 1626, and (in the case of the Library of Congress copy, and that belonging to the Society of Antiquaries) 1627 with varying addresses were used for a new edition of the text, the printed title page of which was always dated 1627. Was there perhaps some delay in producing the second edition so that, although Constable had the engraved title page ready in 1625, 1626, and 1627, Peacham did not supply him with the new text (or Constable did not print it) until 1627? A more complete examination of all available copies may offer some solution, but for the moment it looks very much as though either Peacham's absence in Lincolnshire created some impediment that slowed down a planned second edition or that there was a bookseller's ploy to suggest a new edition (in 1626) when none was meant.

XX   *The Second Edition of 1627: New Material*

More important, perhaps, than these bibliographical complexities is that the second edition of *The Compleat Gentleman* contains two new final chapters, the contents of which are described on the printed title page as "a description of the order of a Maine Battaile, or Pitched Field, eight seuerall wayes: as also certaine necessarie Instructions concerning the Art of Fishing." The title page also refers to further unspecified additions, by which Peacham means the adjustments and new examples added to the chapter on blazonry.[50] The chapter "Of Military Observations" is a very technical set of instructions on military drill, designed to assist in the task of teaching "the *Posture* of each weapon to euery single Souldier." It lacks any vestige of Peacham's personal anecdotal touch, and it would not be in the least surprising to find that it had been borrowed from one of the many military manuals of the day. Certainly it is very similar to parts of both Edward Davies's *The Art of War* (1619) and Gervase Markham's *The Souldiers Accidence* (1625), and it may well have been modelled on either.

The chapter on fishing, by contrast, is more in keeping with the remainder of the book, and begins on a typically personal note: "I haue taken so much delight in the Art of Angling that I may well terme it the honest & patient mans Recreation, or a Pastime for all men to recreat themselues at vacunt howers" (sig. 2H^r). According to Ruth Kelso, this was the first occasion on which fishing had been included in treatises on the education of a noble or gentleman, but that is not to say that it was a new form of leisure activity or that

Peacham was the first to write about it. Indeed, it is clear that Peacham's chapter and the later well-known work of Isaac Walton were preceded by a considerable literature going back as far as *The Boke of Saint Albans* (1496 edition).[51] Peacham's chapter provides a basic lesson on rods, lines, floats, baits, and the characteristics of freshwater fish. It makes an odd ending, and there are no signs that he has given any thought as to how best to integrate his two new chapters into the text of the work as a whole. The conclusion of the chapter on travel retains its indented format as though to mark the end of the book, and its wording is also unaltered so that it opens with the words "I will conclude with *Trauaile*" and ends with Peacham's best wishes for his student's future happiness and success in studies. It certainly is odd that Peacham takes pains to alter details in the chapter on blazonry to account for the recent deaths of Hobart and Sackville but does not bother to reshape the book's conclusion here or in the third edition of 1634.[52] Possibly the explanation is to be found in his distance from London.

XXI The Compleat Gentleman: *Third Edition 1634*

In 1634 a further edition of *The Compleat Gentleman* was published with new chapters "Of Antiquities" and "Of sundry Blazonnes, both Ancient and Modern" inserted into the body of the work,[53] together with a considerable number of new illustrated examples added to the section on "The practice of Blazonry."[54] Some copies were published with a new edition of *The Gentleman's Exercise* appended at the back, and another issue of this edition was available separately in 1634. The most interesting new feature of the 1634 edition is the chapter "Of Antiquities" which deals with sculpture, inscriptions, and coins. Of particular interest is the section on sculpture. During the sixteenth century a few English patrons of the arts had shown some interest in sculpture, but for the real beginnings of English interest in collecting antique statuary we inevitably turn to the purchases of classical works from about 1614 by a small group of wealthy nobility, among them John Digby (1st Earl of Bristol), Sir Kenhelm Digby, George Villiers (Duke of Buckingham), and above all Thomas Howard (Earl of Arundel). Howard went so far as to initiate excavations in Rome, and his finds and purchases were subsequently set up in the galleries and gardens at Arundel house, many of them ultimately finding their way to the Ashmolean Museum, Oxford, where they may still be seen. Other

collectors, including Charles I, later joined in the scramble to trans-
plant Greece and Rome to London, and by the time Peacham wrote
the chapter, collections existed in a number of places in London,
principally at Arundel House, York House, St. James's Palace, and
Somerset House. Peacham points out that those who were knowl-
edgeable about such matters were called "Virtuosi," and he has no
hesitation in recommending that every gentleman, whether or not
he can afford to collect such rarities, should nonetheless be something of a virtuoso. Peacham is the first author in English courtesy
literature to stress that a gentleman should cultivate his taste in such
directions though in this he was perhaps partly influenced, as his
high praise for Thomas Howard implies, by a desire to compliment a
man thought by a number of scholars to have been Peacham's patron, despite lack of evidence that he ever was.

XXII   The Compleat Gentleman: *Fourth Edition 1661*

In 1661, sometime after Peacham's death, a new edition of *The
Compleat Gentleman* was published to which was appended a new
edition of *The Gentleman's Exercise*. The same engraved title page
as for the 1634 edition was used, still with the words "Sculp. Anno
1626," but with the misleading reference to "second Impression"
altered to "Third Impression," "1634" altered to "1661," and the
reference to Francis Constable altered to "for Richard Thrale at the
Cross-Keyes at Saint Paules-gate entring into Cheepside." The title
page plate, engraved by Francis Delarum and originally prepared
for the 1622 edition and used in altered form for subsequent editions
in Peacham's lifetime, thus had a considerable life.

According to "M.S." who addresses the reader at the beginning of
the 1661 edition, Peacham's book had been subjected to "envy, and
unkind censures." This may be an allusion to Richard Brathwaite's
remark in *The English Gentleman* (1630) concerning his own choice
of title: "Now for the *Title*, I am not wholly ignorant, how a subject
intitled *The Complete Gentleman*, was heretofore published; which
(I can assure you *Gentlemen*) consorts with this rather in *Title* than
Tenour, *Name* than *Nature*; the proof whereof I referre to the
generous and judicious Reader" (sig. ¶2ᵛ). Brathwaite's book can be
read as fundamentally opposed to Peacham's, and his similar title
was probably no coincidence. It was Peacham's "consciousness of
superiority and his unquestioning acceptance of the perfection of
the individual as a justifiable end in itself" which, according to W.

Lee Ustick, roused the ire of Brathwaite for whom being a gentleman was primarily a matter of *"goodnesse* of *Person,* than *greatnesse* of *Place,"* and for whom any code of behavior that took no account of the rest of humanity outside one's own circle was unacceptable.[55] Above all, for Brathwaite a gentleman's central goal was the establishment of a proper relationship between himself and his Maker, a matter which indirectly colors almost every topic of discussion. This strong religious preoccupation is in marked contrast to Peacham's stress upon the cultivation of Humanistic studies. Doubtless, there were many who shared Brathwaite's view of Peacham's book in the 1630s, and we certainly know that such attitudes were increasingly inseparable from political allegiances, exacerbated in the years preceding 1661 by the experience of the Civil War.

The 1661 edition of *The Compleat Gentleman* contains a number of additions not by Peacham. These occur chiefly in the section on blazonry, and, as "M.S." explains, the additional families mentioned "are an humble Sacrifice, and duty paid to them, by one who faithfully Honours them for many reasons; but chiefly because they Honour the King." Other additions are made to bring Peacham's allusions to individual families up to date, particularly when they have played some significant role on the Royalist side in the war. For this reason the 1661 edition is very much a Restoration work, its publication being tinged with political overtones that Peacham could never have foreseen. There are also, however, certain other additions, notably a new chapter on "Directions for Painting, or Colouring of Cuts, and printed Pictures in Water-Colours," the author of which is probably Sir Thomas Blount who is believed to have been the author of the section on the Blount family (pp. 230–34). Other minor additions have often been skillfully contrived to give the appearance of being Peacham's. A new paragraph, for example, that concludes the section on the lives of the artists and refers to Franciscus Junius's *De Pictura Veterum* (1637) could easily be taken as Peacham's own, complete with characteristic self-advertisement: "There be several Books extant, in several Languages, concerning this Subject of Painting, Among others, *Fran. Junius, de pictura veterum:* was, not many years agoe, Printed in *London.* And likewise my Book called the *Gentlemans Exercise,* concerning the whole Art of Limming and Painting. The Reader, if he please, may have recourse unto him, for further satisfaction" (pp. 154–55). However, other such passages are more obviously by Blount, who at one point himself inserts an advertisement for one of his books, his *The Art of Making Devises*, a translation of Henri Estienne (p. 277).

The importance of the 1661 edition is, therefore, not that it contains any hitherto unpublished authorial additions but that it establishes the regard with which Peacham's most ambitious work was held in certain circles. By the late 1650s it was considered one "of the Most Vendible Books in England," and shortly after the new 1661 edition appeared, the Lord Chief Justice during a trial implied that it was a work that afforded a familiar model of gentlemanly conduct. Today our interest in this book is of a different kind. Aside from its very special value for historians of art, music, and education, it stands out as an important statement of a Humanist ideal that was born in the sixteenth century and, we now recognize, ultimately came to full fruition in the English school and university system only in the nineteenth century.

CHAPTER 4

Peacham the Poet

PEACHAM wrote poetry all his life. Something has already been said about his various English and Latin emblem verses, his dedicatory verses for a number of his contemporaries' books, and the verses he supplied late in life for a number of Hollar's engravings. It is now time to consider Peacham's two collections of epigrams, his three elegies, and his two celebratory collections of poems.

I *The Epigrams*

The epigram as a poetic genre has always tended to defy any tidy definition. Its most consistent features, however, are brevity, singleness of theme, and, since the time of Martial, its tendency to conclude with some witty or ingenious turn of thought or with some especially pointed summation of its subject-matter. The genre lends itself to an immense variety of tone, since epigrams can be harshly satiric, elegiac, lyrical, adulatory, obscene, or hortatory. They may also be concerned with any number of subjects that include most commonly those of human vices and follies, the deaths of great men, the experience of love, the praise of men, cities, countries, institutions, or some preferred way of life, bawdy anecdotes and witticisms, the urging of some moral *dictum,* and even (as in the case of Richard Crashaw's epigrams) the expression of religious experience. Clearly the essence of the genre lies not so much in its tone or subject-matter, but in its formal and stylistic characteristics—its brevity, its wit, and its methods of creating a pointed ending.

The history of the genre is a long one. When Peacham produced his two collections, he and his English contemporaries had available as their principal models the Planudean anthology—that wonderful anthology of Greek epigrams made in the fourteenth century and first published in 1494; the much more satiric, urbane, and bawdy

91

work of the Latin poet Martial, the epigrammatist most frequently
associated with the pointed ending; the work of various neo-Latin
epigrammatists such as Erasmus, Sir Thomas More, Theodore De
Beza, and George Buchanan; the work of writers in English such as
John Heywood and George Turbervile; and those highly influential
collections by the satiric English epigrammatists of the 1590s.
Peacham's two collections were published in 1608 and 1620 and
hence belong to a period—the first quarter of the seventeenth century—when at least fifty other collections of epigrams found their
way onto the booksellers' stalls. It is consequently hard to believe
the printer's claim, recorded in *The More the Merrier*, Peacham's
first collection, that "Poetrie in this kinde" is "out of request."[1]

II   The More the Merrier

In *The More the Merrier* (1608), his first publication after *The Art
of Drawing*, Peacham seems concerned not to be too closely associated with some of the English epigrammatists who preceded
him, and his signing himself "H.P. *Gent*." and addressing his dedicatee as "M.H.C. *Esquire*" must be seen as means of gaining a
slender degree of protective anonymity.[2] As his dedicatory epistle
to "M.H.C." implies, Peacham was well aware that many epigrams
of the day were either "ouer luscious for obscenitie" or vicious in
their satiric attacks upon private individuals. Consequently, epigrammatists were frequently criticized by guardians of morals and
institutions and by any who believed they had been personally
satirized. Aware of the hazards of prison and the manner in which
books deemed scandalous or seditious were frequently called in and
destroyed, Peacham includes in his dedicatory epistle a denial that
he is guilty of any of his fellows' common faults. Many a writer, of
course, made such denials tongue-in-cheek and almost as a matter of
convention, but in *The More the Merrier* there is no sign that
Peacham indulged in either personal satire or in obscenity, although
Kate's buttocks (Ep. 10) and "euery whoore-house" (Ep. 15) are
subjects blunt enough. Doubtless such topics are partly the cause
for Peacham's apology in Epigram 45: "Be not agreeued my humorous lines affoord/ Of looser language heere and there a word,/ Who
vndertakes to sweepe a common sincke,/ I cannot blame him,
though his besome stincke."

In Epigram 45 Peacham is also alluding to the humble status of
the epigram in his own age, and his epistle "To the Reader" speaks

more openly of this matter: "you cannot esteeme lighter of this stuffe then I doe my selfe" (sig. A3ᵛ). There is an air of the conventional about such self-denigration, and perhaps an apology closer to Peacham's real beliefs is in "To the Reader" where, referring to Erasmus, More, Beza, and others, he says: "For putting pen to paper in this kind, if thou beest truly ingenuous, thou wilt excuse me, when men of better iudgement then either thou, (as I imagine,) or my selfe haue taken paines herein" (sig. A3ʳ).

By far the bulk of Peacham's epigrams in *The More the Merrier* are of a satiric kind, attacking, as the title page and "Ad Musas" insist, the follies of the world. In particular, Peacham singles out prodigality (Ep. 11), women's use of cosmetics (Eps. 6, 39), excessive drinking (Ep. 13), ignorant schoolmasters (Ep. 21), the artful avarice of lawyers (Ep. 40), and society's general lack of esteem for the arts (Ep. 25). All these subjects are topical, but they are also generalized and largely lack the venom of personal invective that one sometimes finds in the epigrams of Peacham's contemporaries. A typical example is Peacham's version of an age-old criticism of one aspect of female vanity: "*Gellia* tis well thou wearst a Mask ith' Sunne,/ For should thy painting thaw thou wert vndone" (Ep. 6).

Other epigrams are concerned with himself and his poetry, matters that a few years later were to provide an important theme in *Minerva Britanna*. Epigram 1, for example, deals humorously with his wit, which he claims to love as much as "Mincio loues his wife,/ Who lately got her carted for a whore." Epigram 43 provides the fascinating self-portrait, quoted already at the beginning of Chapter 1, and Epigram 59 suggests that the fruit of his wit is like that from "the Orenge tree/ Som bloom'd, some green, some ripe som rotte [n] be." He also anticipates *Minerva Britanna* in his concern with the lack of recognition accorded to men of desert:

> *Cyclus* the Souldier, and *Ciuisian*,
> The Pandar, painter and Musitian,
> Saw nothing was be gotten by the artes,
> By wit, by fortune, friendshippe or desertes,
> Hath now a late turnd foole and gotten more
> Then he could doe with all his witte before. [Ep. 25]

Like Martial, who while at Rome nostalgically expressed his hope that his native Bilbilis would be proud of him, Peacham praises his

birthplace, North Mymms, emphasizing its literary associations
with More and Heywood (Ep. 34), and follows Martial in expressing
his preference for a simple country life (Ep. 33). Peacham's sentiments can be related to pastoral convention and may thus be strictly
literary rather than representative of a personal point of view, although they recur often enough in his works to make us suspect that
they reflect his own preferences.[3]

As in his prose works, Peacham's gift for colorful detail, the
humorous anecdote, and the shaft of wit are very much in evidence
in his epigrams. Typical of the first is his portrait of "a Country
Maior,/ In sleeues of red, and in a Fox-furd gowne,/ In's Maiestie"
sitting in a wainscot chair (Ep. 2), or the list of places where Lucius
has written his name, among them the top of Paul's, the bottom of a
wine-pot at Bulls, Hobson's wagon, and "euery whoore-house seel-
ing ore your head" (Ep. 15). Not surprisingly, one of his best anecdotal epigrams (Ep. 21) is at the expense of a member of his own
profession, although it is not clear whether the incident really happened or whether Peacham is exploiting the customary directness of
the epigram which often presents material in the first person as
though from the immediate experience of the narrator:

> A countrey pedant sitting in the Sunne,
> Amongst his boyes thus he examines one,
> Your friendes may see that you haue something got,
> What is, Poeta? quoth the boy, a pot,
> Which ouer hearing as I passed by,
> Vnto his Master turning back (quoth I)
> Whats Latine for yo[u]r Cand-sticke on the shelfe?
> Why Sir (quoth he) that's Latine of it selfe.

As for wit, this is the essence of many an epigram, pariculary those
that imitate Martial's gift for engineering some ingenious turn at the
poem's conclusion, frequently through the employment of paradox,
incongruity, deliberate prior misleading of the reader, or irony.
Peacham's Epigram 23, for example, displays a fine control of
bathos:

> Twise-fiue yeares *Ioue* with *Alcumena* lay,
> Ere shee gat valiant *Hercules* they say:
> So after, now full ten yeares labour past,
> Tha'st got I heare a chopping boy at last.

Equally effective is the carefully fashioned comic surprise of Epigram 37:

> Seuerus hauing ouer-look't my rimes,
> With rugged brow, and cought a dozen times,
> This fellow, saith, hath sure a prettie wit,
> Great pitie thus he hath imployed it.

Such is clearly not the stuff of which great poetry is made, in spite of Martial's claim that there was more truth to life in epigrams than in all the epics put together. Peacham realizes this too. Yet presumably he found in the epigram a form that admirably suited him. Indeed the bulk of his poetry is of the epigram type, the verses for his emblems being frequently indistinguishable in form and manner from those of his epigrams, but concerning this last point there should be no surprise, since in the Renaissance emblem verses were commonly categorized as a form of epigram.[4]

III Thalia's Banquet

Thalia's Banquet (1620) contains 127 epigrams, just over twice as many as *The More the Merrier*, but the difference between the two collections is not solely a matter of size. On the title page of *Thalia's Banquet* and in its dedication to Dru Drury, Peacham develops the conceit that his collection is a banquet "Furnished with an hundred *and odde dishes of newly deu*ised Epigrammes." Drury is invited by Peacham's Muse "to take the praeemenince (as you deserue) and vpper-end of her Table" together with "many worthy *friends*" and "*all that* loue in offensiue mirth." Then the Muse Thalia welcomes "*Euery vnderstanding guest,/ From the* Colledge *and the* Hall," members of the Inns of Court, courtiers, citizens "*that were made/ As well for learning as for trade*," soldiers, ladies, and their attendant maids. The conceit, hardly original, is apt because about a quarter of Peacham's epigrams are tributes to friends and to men and women he admires. Such laudatory tributes to named individuals were a stock-in-trade of the epigrammatist though Peacham had not included any in *The More the Merrier*. Many of the personal tributes in *Thalia's Banquet* are to people Peacham must have met while teaching in Norfolk. That "To Maister *Thomas Townsend* of *Testerton*" (Ep. 63) is typical and seems intended, like a number of others, to provide some gesture of gratitude for hospitality or favors received:

Right worthy sir, for that respect and cheere,
I found at your comparelesse *Testerton,*
With my best friends I do inuite you heere,
Vnto our Muses meane collation.
Which for your bounteous entertaine put downe,
The *only* best housekeeper in your towne.

In addition to such personal tributes are those to men and women whom Peacham may not have known personally but yet admired, among them Michael Drayton, William Byrd, and Alice and Ann Dudley. The epigram addressed to Ben Jonson may serve as an example: "Since more cannot be added to thy Fame,/ Enough tis onely to expresse thy Name" (Ep. 5). Tributes to places or institutions are also included, and where there was only one of these in the earlier collection, here there are four, one of which is again to North Mymms (Ep. 80), another to Wymondham (Ep. 30), one to Trinity College, Cambridge (Ep. 51), and one to the Universities of Oxford and Cambridge (Ep. 56).

Thalia's Banquet retains a quota of satiric epigrams; again we find attacks on prodigality, idle schoolmasters, lawyers, and contemporary disregard for the arts. Peacham expands his gallery of human follies by adding satiric epigrams on upstart poets, Puritans, the rich, courtiers, physicians, and the evils of those who administer benefices unfairly. A further addition is the increased number of bawdy epigrams, in spite of Peacham's assurance on the title page that his mirth is "in offensiue." One wonders how the "nobly-disposed, modest and faire Sisters" (Alice and Ann Dudley) addressed in Epigram 22 would have responded to the *double entendre* in Epigram 124:

Nocturnus who was wont from place to place,
To foote it by his Maisters geldings side,
He dead, his Mistris lik'd so well his pace,
He now at ease doth in the saddle ride.

As before, Peacham displays his talent for the humorous anecdote, the colorful detail, and the sparkling witticism. In general the epigrams in *Thalia's Banquet* show a greater control of language and a more polished wit than those of the earlier collection. Many examples illustrating the quality of these more successful verses spring to mind, but one will suffice. In Epigrams 108 and 109 Peacham recounts an experience in the monastery library at s'Hertogenbosch. While he "was busie perusing some bookes," a friar wrote a Latin distich in Peacham's Greek Testament exploiting the familiar Angelus/Anglia pun attributed to Pope Gregory. The jibe did not go unanswered, and Peacham recounts how, "His back being turn'd, I left this behind me, in the first printed page of a faire *Arias Montanus* bible, to requite him":

> *Ad Syluam Ducis.*
> Why falselie art thou call'd the *Dukes-wood*, when
> Thou hast no woods, and all thy feildes are fenne?
> Thy Trees (I ghesse) are turn'd to sainted stocks,
> And begging Friers haue robb'd thee of thy blocks.

If the anecdote is true, Peacham was no doubt as amusing in life as he can be in his writing, something that is not always true of literary humorists.

IV *The Elegies:* The Period of Mourning

After epigrams and emblems Peacham's largest body of poetry consists of the elegies he wrote on the deaths of Prince Henry, Richard Sackville, and Frances Rich. The term "elegy" was rarely used in the sixteenth century and tended in any case to be applied to a wide variety of types of poetry. Increasingly, however, the term was used of funeral poems or verses intended to commemorate a particular deceased person.[5] During the seventeenth century this type of poem developed as a quite distinctive genre, and, as Ruth Wallerstein, Robert Cawley, and others have noted, it was the flood of such poems on the death of Prince Henry that really established the genre.[6]

The status of Prince Henry in the minds of the English at large was an extraordinary phenomenon that has probably never been repeated in the history of the British monarchy. In this very young man were vested the hopes and dreams of a nation. Certainly Henry was a remarkable youth—he died when only eighteen—but to some extent he had his virtues thrust upon him. Partly out of disenchantment with James I, Englishmen lauded Henry as the ideal prince, associating him with all the traditional regal virtues. With his love of chivalry he seemed like a reincarnation of the Elizabethan age, and much was made of the fact that he was Queen Elizabeth's godson.

He seemed the perfect combination of soldier, scholar, and patron of the arts. His love of ships and special concern for the navy were legendary, his interest in discovery and colonization was much talked of, and his care for the Protestant religion seemed to promise much. In consequence of all this his court at Richmond attracted many learned and gifted men, and his palace by the Thames became a focal point for British aspirations of all kinds. His sudden death in 1612 understandably shocked the nation deeply, since at one stroke Great Britain was deprived of both heir apparent to the throne and of a potent mythical faith in the wonderful future reign of King Henry IX.

Numerous poets poured forth their tributes in elegies which not surprisingly tend to stress three of Henry's characteristics: his status as a warrior—Henry is variously compared to Mars, Achilles, Alexander the Great, King Arthur, the Black Prince, and King Henry V; his love of learning and the arts; and his potential as defender of the Protestant faith. "An Elegiacke Epitaph" in Peacham's *The Period of Mourning* (1613) provides a concise summation of all three prevailing themes when Henry is described as

> The richest Iemme ere *Nature* wrought
> For prizeles forme, of purest thought,
> For chast desire, for Churches zeale,
> For care and loue of common weale;
> For manly shape, for actiue might,
> For Courage and Heroique sprit,
> For Loue of Armes and Heauenly Arts,
> For Bounty toward all best deserts. [sig. D 2^{v}]

Whether Henry would ever have come up to the expectations of his countrymen is impossible to know. Francis Bacon, in typical judicious fashion, says in his *In Henricum Principem Walliae Elogium:* "Many points there were indeed in this prince's nature which were obscure, and could not be discovered by any man's judgement, but only by time, which was not allowed him. Those however which appeared were excellent; which is enough for fame." More skeptically, however, he also wrote that Henry was indeed "a favourer of learning, though rather in the honour he paid it than the time he spent upon it."[7]

It is not certain when precisely Peacham wrote *The Period of Mourning*, but its publication in 1613 did not follow immediately upon Henry's funeral. The work was entered in the Stationer's Register on 8 February, 1613, some three months after the Prince's death, and when it appeared, its title page announced that the volume also included "Nuptiall Hymnes" in honor of the marriage of the Count Palatine and Princess Elizabeth, Prince Henry's sister. This event occurred on 14 February, and, since the volume also contains a description of "THE MANNER OF the Solemnization of this *Royall Marriage*," one must assume that publication did not occur until after that day. Peacham may have felt some unease at combining tears for one event with joy for another, but he does what he can to imply that his elegiac tributes were written well before the *Nuptiall Hymnes*. He appends to *The Period*, for example, an Epecide (a poem "propper to the body while it is vnburied") which he follows with an Epitaph described as having been "Written by the Author, at the time of his [i.e. Henry's] DEATH," and in his dedication to Sir John Swinnerton, Sir Thomas Middleton, and Sir John Iolles, he says that the verses for Prince Henry had been composed "some while since" (sig. A3ᵛ). He also feels called upon to elaborate a rather tasteless conceit, comparing his reminder of Henry's death at the time of his sister's wedding to the ancient custom of Ethiopian princes "amid their Feasts and Royall Banquets, to haue the head of a dead man laid in Earth, presented the first to the Table; in abundance of Mirth to put them in minde of *Mortalitie*" (sig. A3ʳ).

   The Period of Mourning consists principally of six "Visions" of varying lengths, but all in *Venus and Adonis* stanza form. In them Peacham permits the influence of Spenser to have full play in form, style, and subject-matter. It is clear, for example, that he was familiar with Spenser's paraphrases from Petrarch and Du Bellay, and his decision to employ six visions is probably a conscious imitation of Petrarch. Cawley has listed a number of striking ways in which Peacham echoes Spenser's visions and other poems.[8] In Vision I, for example, Peacham's ship "whose Sayles were Silke, and Tackle twined/ That seem'd reflected, gloriously to guild/ The waue around" is not unlike that in stanza 2 of Spenser's *The Visions of Petrarch* with its "sailes of golde, of silke the tackle were," and both ships are destroyed in similar fashion on rocks. In Vision II Peacham depicts a palm tree "Wherein all kindes of singing Birds did build,/ Melodiously reioycing euermore," and this is not unlike a passage in Vision 3 of *The Visions of Petrarch* depicting a laurel tree in which

"Such store of birds therein yshrowded were,/ Chaunting in shade
their sundrie melodie." Peacham's tree is felled by a serpent "That
vndermin'd the Body night and day,/ That last, it downe with hid-
eous fragor fell," while Spenser's laurel is struck by lightning. However, in Vision 7 of "Visions of the Worlds Vanitie" Spenser depicts
a cedar that is destroyed by a "litle wicked worme," and Peacham
may have taken his cue from this. Further echoes could be mentioned, but one more will suffice. In Vision VI Peacham describes a
journey to Elysium:

> Within there was a Theater of gold,
> Rais'd on a mount in semi-circle wise,
> Which stately columnes strongly did vphold,
> That by ascent did ouer other rise,
>   And railde betweene with Christall lights that shone
>   Against the Sunne like Rockes of Diamond. [sig. C 2^r]

Spenser in Vision 2 of *The Visions of Bellay* has the following:

> On high hills top I saw a stately frame,
> An hundred cubits high by iust assize,
> With hundreth pillours fronting faire the same,
> All wrought with Diamond after Dorick wize:
> Nor brick, nor marble was the wall in view,
> But shining Christall, which from top to base
> Out of her womb a thousand rayons threw,
> On hundred steps of *Afrike* golds enchase.

Here, as in the instances mentioned in Chapters 2 and 3, Peacham
shows that he was not averse to imitating and echoing Spenser, and
in doing so he joins Giles and Phineas Fletcher, George Wither,
William Browne, and others who maintained the Spenserian manner well into the seventeenth century.[9]

In Peacham's Vision I the poet describes seeing "A goddly Arke"
called *Archôn*. This wonderful craft, we quickly infer, is in part a
poetic evocation of the *Prince Royal*, the largest ship built in England to that time, and a ship that Prince Henry christened himself at
her launching in Woolwich in 1610. Peacham's *Archôn* is also symbolic, however, of Prince Henry himself, a peerless prince about to
set out in life, the hopes of the nation with him in the days following
his creation as Prince of Wales. Nor are the Prince's special interests

in the arts, in military matters, and in exploration and colonization
forgotten by Peacham:

> She *Archôn* hight, for that she had no Peere,
> And could command the *Ocean* with her might:
> In whom the Hopes of many thousands were,
> But chiefly of the Muse, and Martiall sprite:
>> Braue Man of warre she was, from *Britaine* bound,
>> For new discoueries all that might be found. [sig. B 1^r]

The "goodly Arke" is then wrecked, and Peacham uses the disaster
to comment on the fate of those who had been dependent on
Henry's patronage, his own grief, and the fate of Great Britain at
large ("A fraught wherein we shared euery one,/ And by whose losse
three Kingdomes are vndone").

In the second Vision the Prince is symbolized by a palm tree.
Three great crowns (presumably those of the three kingdoms) weigh
it down—"For little wot we managing of Realmes,/ The howerly
cares and charge of Diadems"—and on every bough sit "all kindes of
singing Birds" (presumably writers and poets) which rejoice "In his
deere aide, by whom they were vpheld." Again disaster strikes, this
time in the form of "a fearefull Serpent" (Henry's fatal illness) "That
vndermin'd the Body night and day,/ That last, it downe with hid-
eous fragor fell." The third Vision also takes up the theme of death,
and, echoing Spenser's description of the Cave of Despair, Peacham
represents the Cave of Death. Death himself, "a meagre wretch
alone/ That had in sorrow both his ei'n outwept,/ And was with pine
become a Sceleton," is not unlike Spenser's Despair whose "raw-
bone cheekes" are the result of "penurie and pine." Death explains
that he is "Perplexed here, for *Henries* losse of breath," and at this
point Peacham develops an unusual conceit. Instead of declaiming
against death, as had so many other elegiasts,[10] he defends him and
makes Death himself a mourner. Apparently Death's arrow has mis-
carried, and in sorrow for his error Death is now "Perplexed here,
for *Henries* losse of breath." Henry's untimely end was "against his
will;/ For who knew *Henry* could not meane him ill."

In Vision IV Peacham portrays the transformation of a golden
triumphal chariot drawn by four lions ("Three of England and that
one of Scotland") and driven by Vna (Unity), "a Virgin, louely to
behold." In the chariot is "a warlick Impe" (Henry) "Who *Phoebus*,
in his glorious armes out-shone,/ Ydrad of all for awfull Maiestie,/

Yet louing, and more loued liued none." A fiery wand from Heaven
turns all to black, the chariot becomes Henry's funeral hearse, and
Peacham presents the funeral procession, including the telling detail of Henry's "gallant Steede that did disdaine the bit,/ And shooke
with angry hoofe the hollow ground,/ His Riders losse lamented
ouer it."[11]

Vision V by contrast is in a pastoral vein. The poet, sitting close to
two tributaries of the Thames, hears an Orpheus-like voice lament-
ing the death of Dion. In a series of similes the grief for Dion/
Henry's loss to Albion (Britain) is said to be far greater than that of
Philomela's loss of her young, Calliope's of Homer, and Venus's of
Adonis. Then comes one of Peacham's finest moments. The theme is
conventional, but its expression is quite moving due chiefly to its
controlled rhythms and the carefully contrived "dying" cadence of
the final couplet:

> If in a garden but the Mallow die,
> The Daisie, Dill, or Rose, it liues agen,
> And shooteth yeerely from his bed on high,
> But we endu'de with Reason who are men,
>   Much fairer, stronger, if we once doe fall,
>   No more on Earth our being haue at all. [sig. C1ʳ]

A series of heraldic animals and birds, representing various noble
families, come to lament the loss of Dion, but in the very effective
last line the poet is "left to mourne disconsolate alone."

Whereas in the third Vision the poet had discovered the Cave of
Death, in the sixth and final Vision he is conducted to Elysium "by a
louely childe,/ Whose haire outshone the brightest burning gold."
There the poet sees many dead kings and references are made
(accompanied by copious marginalia) to the various young English
princes who died before they inherited the crown. Henry is enthroned and "rais'd higher then the rest," and the poem thus ends
on a note of consolation further emphasized by the notion that Princess Elizabeth and Prince Charles are living reflections of their dead
brother's glory.

The Visions are followed by a four-page Epicede, an altogether
less attractive poem in octosyllabic couplets. Possibly Peacham actually wrote it during the few days between the Prince's death and
his burial, its general triteness being the consequence of haste. To
this Peacham appends six lines of equally undistinguished verse "To

the buried Prince," and there follows "An Elegiacke Epitaph" supposedly written at the time of the death. The Epitaph is a competent, formal elegy, full of such conventional (though by no means ineffectual) motifs as "For Griefe her selfe is stricken dumbe" or "by Teares of yet vnborne,/ His Marble wilbe wash'd and worne." Henry, it is said, has gone to his new coronation and is now free from vain and parasitical courtiers. From Heaven he looks down, "And bid'st Adieu these heapes of clay,/ Cares restles roomes, Innes for a day." The poem ends on a note of apt hyperbole, tinged no doubt with a modicum of sincere grief: "But till my death I weare my dayes/In Zealous teares, and in thy praise,/ Since I may neuer lieu to see/ A *Prince*, or *Henrie*, like to thee." Greek and Latin epitaphs by Peacham's learned friend John Selden are then unexpectedly followed by four emblematic Latin poems by Peacham, each accompanied by a woodcut illustration: the prince's crown, his Prince of Wales crest, the Tudor rose, and the Scottish thistle. The volume then concludes with three Latin funeral epigrams, a common type of epigram but one not previously employed anywhere by Peacham.

V *The Elegies:* An Aprill Shower

Sometime in or shortly before 1622, Peacham inserted some extra pages in *The Compleat Gentleman* while it was being printed in order to praise Richard Sackville, the Earl of Dorset, and indirectly to express gratitude for favors received. It seems reasonable to assume that Peacham had only recently begun to benefit from Sackville's generosity, but, for the second time in his life, Peacham was shortly deprived of his new patron through death, Sackville dying suddenly on 28 March, 1624. Within three weeks Peacham had composed an elegy, which he entitled *An Aprill Shower* and dedicated to Anne Sackville, the earl's widow. One suspects that Peacham may well have hoped that she would continue to assist him in some way, even though he is careful to state that "it is no by-regard,/ Or expectation of a slight reward/ Enforces me to weepe" (sig. B1^v).

An Aprill Shower (1624) begins with a Latin epitaph and a twelve-line "Monument to the Reader." In this latter Peacham develops the conceit that Dorset's body is "but the Case/ Wherein this precious Iewell was" which now lodges in the register of Fame, the hearts of friends, and in Heaven. Dorset is immortal, "For though

with mee his dust doth lie,/ Beleeue it, DORSET cannot Die" (sig.
A1^v). The elegy itself follows, consisting of just over one hundred
and fifty lines of decasyllabic couplets. In general the quality of the
verse is distinctly below that in *The Period of Mourning*. Frequently
its rhythms are stilted, its manner overcontrived, and its emotional
tone lacking in conviction. Lines like the following are common:

> . . . The common losse
> Of KING, and COVNTREY, calls to beare their crosse
> And so I will; know then whom wee haue lost,
> Euen him, whom Artes and Armes may truely boast
> To bee their owne. Wee tricke not his Discent
> And Images, which in our COMPLEMENT,
> Who list may view at large; . . . [sig. B1^v][12]

The poem presents an idealized portrait of the Earl as "Reli-
giously inclin'd" and Charitable ("By adding Stipends to your Liu-
ings small,/ Maintaining many who had none at all"). Dorset is said
to be devoid of "haughtie-brow'd Disdayne," never denying "ac-
cesse euen to the Childe." He is an enemy "to garish Pride and
Fashion,/ The *Epilepsie* of our English Nation," except when "His
Prince did call vpon his Seruice, then/ Stout DIOMEDE in Armes,
not brighter shone,/ Or man more Glorious was to looke vpon." He
is learned, a "Rare Poet," a "great MOECENAS of all Poesie," and
constant in friendship. Here indeed is someone approaching
Peacham's own conception of a complete gentleman, and it is no
accident, we may be sure, that the passage describing the Earl's
"plainest plaine" clothes of "Ciuill blacke of Rash, of Serge, or so,/
The Liuerie of wise Stayednesse" and his very different dress when
called upon to serve his prince echoes Peacham's earlier laudatory
description in *The Compleat Gentleman* of the "blacke or sad stuffe"
worn by Charles V "except in times of warre" and on the necessity
for a gentleman to "spare not to be braue with the brauest" when he
represents his prince.[13]

In addition to these many supposed virtues, Sackville is com-
plimented for the hospitality at Knole, his house in Sevenoaks,
Kent. Here Peacham briefly places himself alongside a number of
contemporaries, notably Jonson and Andrew Marvell, who composed entire poems in praise of particular country houses.
Peacham's lines do not perhaps match the excellence of "To Pens-

hurst" or "Upon Appleton House," but they are nonetheless among
the best in the poem and sufficiently polished to earn Peacham his
place in the history of the country house poem:

> What State, what Traine, what Order, House kept hee
> At his faire KNOWLE, a Paradise to mee
> That seem'd for site, a Court for greatest Prince,
> The Home of *Honour*, and *Magnificence;*
> Where every day a Christmasse, seem'd, that fed
> The neighbour Poore, that else had famished.
> How did his Loue and Noblest Care extend
> To all his followers, at his latter end
> I need not tell, themselues will say for mee,
> Men neuer seru'd a better Lord then hee. [sig. B3ʳ]

It would appear that Peacham knew "To Penshurst" which had been
published eight years earlier in 1616. Certainly his poem displays a
close similarity to Jonson's central theme which G. R. Hibbard has
defined as "the function of the house in the community as the centre
of a complex web of relationships which makes up the fabric of
civilisation."[14] Hibbard credits Jonson with establishing the tradition of the country house poem in England, but in noting a number
of imitations of Jonson's poem he does not mention Peacham's small
contribution. Yet clearly Peacham was at his best when working
with someone else's book open in front of him, and fortunately he
tended to select for imitation only the best writers.

An Aprill Shower concludes with three short poems. The first
consists of two Visions in rhyme royal, for which Peacham returns to
his beloved Spenser. The first Vision portrays "A louely Nymph, her
wiery-golden haire/ Sit rending, wayling that faire place beside."
She represents Religion and is sitting by the River Stour close to
Canterbury (the seat of the Anglican primate) mourning the loss of
Dorus (i.e. Dorset) "Whose loue I had, and hee my heart againe."
Peacham's original is to be found in the opening of Spenser's *The
Ruines of Time* where another nymph sits beside the "siluer
streaming *Thamesis*" sorrowfully "wailing,/ Rending her yeolow
locks, like wyrie golde." In the second Vision Peacham describes "a
goodly Lawrel, streight and Greene,/ Vpon whose top sweet singing
Birds did build." This is very similar to the palm described in *The
Period of Mourning* but this time it is much more closely modelled
on Spenser's laurel tree in *Visions of Petrarch.* Spenser's beautiful

tree is destroyed by lightning, but Peacham instead has his tree felled by "the enuious owner." As before, the tree represents Peacham's patron and the birds are the poets he supports.

As he turned the pages of *The Period of Mourning*, Peacham no doubt came across his short six-line poem "To the buried Prince" which he now rewrites. In the earlier version he compares the manner in which "from each angle of the Vault" of King Henry VII's chapel in Westminster "a line is brought/ Vnto the Kingly founders heart" with the way in which "our loues doe runne by line,/ And dead, concenter in thy [i.e. Prince Henry's] Shrine." The same simile is now polished to appear in "To the Deceased Lord," Peacham making the convenient substitution of Richard Sackville for Henry Stuart (sig. B4ʳ). The volume concludes with an envoy expressing the conventional literary thought that the poet's muse is interred with the dead man,[15] and, just as those attending Spenser's burial cast into his tomb funeral elegies and the pens with which they had been written, Peacham figuratively casts his pen into Dorset's grave: "Noblest DORSET, dead and gone,/ Thy Muse with Poësie haue done:/ And in his Graue, now throwne thy Pen,/ Sit downe and neuer rise agen" (sig. B4ᵛ).

VI   *The Elegies:* Thestylis Atrata

Peacham attempted no further elegies for ten years, until the death in 1634 of Frances Rich, the Dowager Countess of Warwick. Then, Peacham explains to his readers, he "adventured once againe with ORPHEUS to raise up EURIDICE, my dead and forgotten Muse." The result was *Thestylis Atrata: Or A Funeral Elegie Vpon the Death of the Right Honourable, most Religious and Noble Lady, Frances, Late Countess of Warwick.* Peacham was teaching in Lincolnshire in the period 1624 to 1635, and it was there that he probably first made the acquaintance of the Countess. In his "Epistle to the Reader" he speaks warmly of "the many favors I formerly received from her Honour" (sig. A3ʳ), and her regard for Peacham's talents must have been considerable for he mentions in his dedicatory epistle to the Countess's three nephews that "Some few yeares agoe, her Honour sent unto me, and requested mine advice, for the erecting of a Monument in SNARFORD Church for her selfe," Snarford being about ten miles northeast of Lincoln. Peacham duly "drew the Modell of one," adding "(as was her desire) a plaine, but short and proper Inscription, leaving underneath a space for an

Epitaph, there to be inserted after her death, that might containe some dozen lines or more, which (if I should out-live her) it pleased her Honour to impose upon me to performe" (sig. A2^{r-v}). The Countess, however, later changed her mind regarding "the disposing of her corps at the time of her death (for some reasons perhaps knowne unto her selfe)" (sig. A2^v), and Peacham consequently was never to see his design for a monument put into effect, nor was he able to supply the promised epitaph for her tomb. *Thestylis Atrata,* as Peacham explains in his dedication, is his alternative offering, written in what leisure hours he could find while "being employed in a toilsome calling" (presumably teaching).

Peacham's "Funerall Elegie" is prefaced by a Latin epitaph, set out on the page exactly as it might have appeared on the Countess's tomb, beginning with the conventional "Hic jacet" formula, and displaying at its conclusion Peacham's love of anagrams in a curious "Chronogramma numerale" in which key letters in a sentence are capitalized to form the Roman numerals for 1634: "In eXtreMo IVDICIo, IeVs sIt tIbI IesVs./M. DC. XXXIIII" (sig. A4^r). The elegy itself is eight pages long in decasyllabic couplets. As in the elegy for Sackville, there is considerable praise for the personal character of the deceased person, and in this instance the countess's piety, charity, and humility are particularly stressed. Equal praise, however, is lavished upon her public virtues and the manner in which she fulfilled the responsibilities of her noble birth. According to Peacham, she was well educated "in everie Science that was rare, / And commendable Art, that might concerne,/ Or suited with Nobilitie to learne" (sig. B4^v), and, like Sackville, she was a model of hospitality: "Her owne faire SNARFORD, second unto none,/ For site, delight, sweet contemplation,/ At home detain'd her, keeping open dore/ To neighbours, strangers, and the needie poor" (sig. B4^v). Her care for her tenants is several times mentioned, and she is compared to Augustus in her ability and willingness "To lay by state, and conversant to be/ With Tenants, parling of good husbandrie" (sig. C2^r).

Her charity was apparently not confined to her immediate environment (sig. C1^r), and Peacham mentions the endowments she made for preachers, the exhibitions she provided at Magdalen College, Cambridge, and her financial assistance to the hospital at Market Raison, Lincolnshire. Little wonder, then, that Peacham feels able to open his poem with a portrayal of the widespread sense of loss caused by her death: "A losse wherein so many had a share,/ That Townes and Tenants well-nigh undone are" (sig. B1^r). The city of Lincoln itself is among the chief mourners:

> A losse for which faire LINCOLNE from her hill,
> Doth to her Citie streames of teares distill;
> It weepes, and by her River doth convay
> Her salt-abundant sorrow everie way;
> And as a Mother, who hath lately lost
> Her dearest daughter, whom with care and cost,
> She from her tender infancie hath bred,
> And in all goodly Science nurtured:
> With bitter teares, and wringing oft her hands,
> Amidst her neighbours dumb and sobbing stands,
> Incapable of comfort, and would faine,
> Even with her fingers dig her up againe: . . . [sig. B1^{r-v}]

Peacham then engages in a lengthy catalogue of various past worthies of Lincolnshire, including the Countess's father. As with the extended simile just quoted, he may be imitating a device common in epic, but here the introduction of his catalogue seems forced—a mere excuse for the antiquary to parade his knowledge—and the unity of the poem is seriously disturbed. Because Peacham's list of worthies contains many unfamiliar names, he feels called upon to insert lengthy prose annotations directly into the body of the text, thereby further disrupting the flow of the verse. Consequently, the elegy proper does not return to its true course for some seven pages when Peacham, as well he might, pauses to say: "But what availes all this, it is not Bloud,/ Alliance, Honours, Fortunes make us good" (sig. B4^v).

Once Peacham refocuses upon his subject, the quality of his verse improves, and his skill with the rhyming couplet in particular shows a marked improvement over his earlier poems. Three sections of the remainder of the elegy provide sufficient examples to demonstrate the point, and they are quoted here at some length because they probably represent Peacham's poetry at its best. The first such passage occurs when Peacham is praising the Countess's hospitality and her preference for remaining at a country residence. Its manner differs greatly from the Spenserian verse of which he was so fond, and in it we can sense instead a minor poet's competent anticipation of the brilliance later to characterize Swift, Dryden, or Pope:

> Now blush (yee Dames) who leave your Mansions faire,
> The fragrant fields, the healthfull Countrey aire,
> Your walks, your woods, your flowrie gardens sweet,
> To live immur'd within a stinking street,
> Exchanging your all-welcome giving gates
> For some small wicket, fit to breake our pates;
> T'avoid expences, spending, and to flie
> Your Countries, but for hospitalitie:
> Or learne what fashion most is in request,
> How is this Countesse, that Court Ladie drest;
> While yee, your beauteous faces so disguise,
> We neither see your foreheads, nor your eyes:
> (Like Dutch Boores houses, where the straw hangs over
> The low-thatcht eaves, and doth the windowes cover)
> That wont the seats and *Indices* to be
> Of Spirit, Love, and Ingenuitie. [sig. C1^r][16]

Equally effective, but this time on the theme of Vanity, is a group of passages in the final pages of the elegy. Women's overconcern with beauty is the first target:

> See (Ladies) what it is that make you proud,
> A verie nothing, an IXIONS cloud,
> When most belov'd, pursu'd, embrac'd and kist,
> Dissolves it selfe to vapor and to mist:
> A blushfull blossome, pleasing to the eye,
> No sooner blowne, but blasted by and by. [sig. C3^r]

This develops into a more general portrait of Death the Great Leveller:

> *Death's* King of *Heraulds* overlooking tombs,
> At Church all placing in their proper roomes,
> All marshalling at Funerals and Feasts,
> Ranking with all equalitie his guests.
> And Ladies, see, that commonly contend
> For highest place at Church, or Tables end;
> How quickly can this enemie of life
> Decide the quarrell, and compound your strife.
> Death's *Harbinger*, the King of Heaven doth send,
> To see you lodged at your progresse end. [sigs. C3^{r-v}]

Towards the conclusion of the elegy, after describing the Countess's death, Peacham imagines her "From the Earths prison now

exempt and free." As she looks back at the earth below, she per-
ceives the triviality of human activity:

> Adieu yee *Courts,* but *Cotes* of clay and stone,
> Whose Turrets now, (me thinks) I tread upon;
> And as an Ant-hill, view the world below;
> Mark how you silly creatures, to and fro,
> Doe toile your selves within your poore abodes,
> By taking up, then laying downe your loads,
> When shortly comes the owner with a spade,
> And layes all levell, what your care hath made. [sigs. C4^{r-v}]

Such lines contain numerous commonplaces, but Peacham's couplets give to the familiar a freshness that commands our attention as
effective verse should.

One last example from *Thestylis Atrata* may serve to demonstrate
Peacham's achievement in this poem. Again it occurs toward the
end of the elegy, but it is quite separate from the satiric passages on
"All is Vanity." It describes the Countess's death following a moving
deathbed scene in which she blesses her friends and servants.
Peacham's simile is borrowed from Vergil, but his anglicized version
in its new context is no less affecting because of our awareness of the
parallel description of Pallas's body in the *Aeneid:*

> This said, of all (while all stand weeping by)
> She takes her leave, and so doth sweetly dye.
> Even as the *Hiacynth* doth change the hue,
> Which (from the tender stalk where late it grew)
> Some Virgins daintie finger off hath torne,
> And that sweet tincture which did it adorne,
> Not fully faded, by degrees doth dye,
> Where some small remnant still affects the eye:
> Even so a colour lifelesse doth she keepe,
> And lovely seemes, as one but fast asleepe. [sig. C4^{r}][17]

The superiority of such verses is obvious, but unfortunately the
potential Peacham displayed in *Thestylis Atrata* never developed
and he wrote no further large-scale poetic work, his remaining
poetry consisting of the verses he contributed to Hollar's engravings. However, two further major poems by Peacham of earlier
dates have yet to be discussed. Quite distinct in kind from the

epigrams and the elegies, they may be categorized as celebratory poems. The first is concerned with a marriage, the second with a birth.

VII   Nuptiall Hymnes: In Honour of the Marriage

Peacham combined his elegy on Prince Henry with a poetic celebration of the marriage of Henry's sister, Elizabeth, to the Count Palatine. There are four *Nuptiall Hymnes* in all, each in a different meter, and all but the first accompanied by Peacham's typically copious marginalia. The first hymn is a rather undistinguished poem of five stanzas, each of which contains eight lines rhyming alternately. It forms a necessary transition from the preceding elegy, making much of the contrast between the season of Winter, which coincided with the Prince's death, and the present season of Spring, which three months later aptly accompanies the Princess's Valentine's Day wedding.

The second hymn consists of sixteen couplets, each line containing seven syllables, a difficult tripping meter that succeeds in some measure in expressing the excitement of the "Nymphes of Sea and Land" as they prepare the bride: "Bring yee Rubies for her Eare,/ Diamonds to fill her Hayre,/ Emrald greene and Chrisolite/ Binde her Necke more white then white" (sig. F1^r). The third hymn describes the bride's progress to the bridal chamber and the joys of marriage. Each of the eighteen stanzas contains two octosyllabic couplets followed by the chorus "Io Hymen Hymenaeus"; they are undistinguished except that they proved in part prophetic: "That one day we may liue to see,/ A *Frederick Henry* on her knee" (sig. F2^v). The fourth and final hymn is much longer, and much more successful as poetry than any of the preceding three. Written in decasyllabic couplets and heavily annotated in places, it first describes the idyllic home of Venus in Cyprus. Peacham's imagination here comes to life and along with it the quality of some of his verses:

> Where still the fields with veluet-greene are spred,
> And blossomes paint the woods all white and red,
> No Bird may perch her on the tender bow
> But such for voyce as *Venus* shall allow.
> The trees themselues doe fall in loue with either,
> As seemes by kissing of their tops together:
> And softly whispring; when some gentle gale
> Chides from the Mountaine, through the shady Vale. [sig. F3^r]

Cupid arrives to ask the goddess to join Frederick and Elizabeth in
marriage, and, accompanied by "Sea-gods, Tritons, Nymphs," she
hastens to England.[18] When she arrives at the "Royall Hall," she
commands that "Affaires of State, ambitious difference,/ Com-
plaints, and Faction, melancholy Feares,/ All Parsimonie, sighes,
and former Teares" be banished, and she orders the hall to be
suitably decorated while she secretly instructs the Princess "how to
loue" (sig. G2[r]). After Venus has praised the Princess's beauty, the
Hymn concludes with the goddess's good wishes for the future and
her hope that the marriage will be fruitful:

> *Liue Roiall Paire* in peace and sweetest Loue,
> With all aboundance blest by heauen aboue,
> A thousand kisses binde your harts together,
> Your Armes be weary with embracing either,
> And let me liue to see betweene you twaine,
> A *Caesar* borne as great as *Charlemaine*. [sig. G3[a]]

The volume then closes with one of John Selden's typically complex
Latin poems, even more heavily annotated than any of the preceding poems by Peacham, while Peacham's concluding journalistic
prose description of the marriage is in curious contrast to the poetic
hyperbole that characterizes the poems themselves.

VIII   Prince Henrie Revived

When the Princess Elizabeth duly produced the young Prince
Henry Frederick in 1614, Peacham celebrated the event with a
genethliacon which he dedicated to the Princess and prefaced with
an engraved portrait of the child. In his dedication Peacham mentions that Elizabeth has earlier taken "notice of me, and my
labours," and a few pages on he refers to the "sweet supportance"
which Elizabeth has given to his verses (sig. A4[r]). Peacham apparently planned to reach her in Heidelberg, present his work to her in
person, and presumably receive further tokens of her favor, but, as
he explains, the route proved to be too dangerous. Peacham's desire
to please Princess Elizabeth is evident in his dedicatory poem to
her. In six Spenserian stanzas he talks first of how the death of
Elizabeth's brother caused him to lay his "reedes for euermore
away." Henry's death was like the passing of the Golden Age of
Queen Elizabeth since simultaneously all proper regard for poetry
disappeared:

> Where are the Summers when the righteous Maid,
> With ev'nest hand the heauenly Scale did weild,
> And golden Deed with golden meed repaid:
> When Vertue was in price, for Vertue, held,
> When Honours daintie but desert did guild,
> And Poesie in graces goodly seene,
> Rais'd her high thought, with straines that Nectar still'd?
> They are ascended with that glorious Queene:
> And she, alas, forgot, as she had neuer beene. [sig. A3ᵛ]

The birth of a second Henry has, however, reawakened Peacham's Muse and promises hope for a new Golden Age: "And Royall child, who like another Sunne,/ From Rosie bed arised'st in the East,/ When that great light we saw extinct and done,/ Ah *Henrie*, waild of euery gentle brest" (sig. A4ᵛ).

Peacham's twenty-page poem then begins. It is in the loftiest style he ever attempted, and begins appropriately with an evocation to his Muse. The verse is in decasyllabic couplets and heavily weighted with mythological, classical, and historical allusions, although Peacham's marginalia are for once conspicuously brief. Some of his couplets, as Margaret Pitman suggests, "would have done justice to the works of 'those first refiners of our numbers,' Waller and Denham."[19] The description of the public celebrations of Henry Frederick's birth is an example: "When Piles bright burning, by the silent Moone/ In euery street, of midnight made the noone,/ While siluer bels, with iron tongues proclaime/ A new borne *Henry*, to the Nymphes of *Thame*" (sig. B2ʳ).

The themes of the poem center around the joyous anticipation accompanying the Prince's nativity. He is "that strong arme expected long agoe,/ Should giue the *Byzant* beast a deadly blow" (sign. B1ᵛ). Not only will he "chase the Crescent from our Hemispheare," but he will bring peace to Christendom, so long the victim of factious schism and war (sig. B3ʳ). Throughout the poem Henry Frederick is equated with a host of mythological heroes, biblical patterns of excellence, and ideal rulers. He will be a Numa or a Solomon in piety and wisdom, a Caesar or a Charlemagne in military leadership, an Alphonsus or James I in learning, and, of course, "A new borne *Henry*" (sig. B2ʳ). His ancestors are praised, especially "*Eliza* Queene, the Maiden conqueresse," the victor over the Spanish Armada in 1588 (sig. C2ʳ). Fundamental to the whole scheme of the poem, however, is Peacham's portrayal of the ideal prince, an interesting anticipation of his views on the ideal gentleman that he published some seven years later. A prince should be peace-loving, he claims, but he should also be the martial hero when need arises:

> But if braue Impe, by *Mars* thou shalt be hent
> From thy soft Pallace, to a warlike tent,
> To vndergoe an honourable war,
> In common, or thine owne particular.
> Then shine in glorious armes Heauen be thy speed,
> And endlesse *Fame* thy euerlasting meed. [sigs. B4^v–C1^r]

Religion must be the "first groundworke" of his education, since Piety is the most important of virtues, but other virtues must receive their due, including Justice, Temperance, Prudence, Clemency, Modesty, and Liberality. The importance of learning, as we would expect, is given special emphasis, along with a prince's responsibility to support the arts (sig. C4^v), and all is finally summed up when Peacham utters that oft-repeated *cri de coeur* of his age: "Oh heauens! to men yee giue no worldly thing/ More pretious then the iust and pious King:/ Vpon whose brow we may estamped see/ The Image of the highest Maiestie" (sig. D2^r).

Perhaps Peacham hoped that the hyperbole he lavishes in this poem on the child would earn him an invitation from the parents to assist in the prince's education. If he did, he was to be disappointed, and for the next five years at least he was confined to an obscure country town in Norfolk with "neuer ceasing toile" at the Free School in Wymondham "which whiles that it was free,/ My selfe the Maister lost my libertie."[20]

* * *

It is not easy to sum up Peacham's poetic achievements. Certainly his verses contain much that is competent and felicitous, but no one could argue that he should be placed among poets of the first rank. He seems most comfortable when writing in the Spenserian manner, but his epigrams and his increasingly skillful use of the rhymed couplet suggest directions in which his development as a poet may have led had Peacham not largely turned aside from poetry and concentrated his talents upon prose.

CHAPTER 5

Peacham the Essayist
and Pamphleteer

I N 1635, after completing his three years of teaching at Heighington School, Peacham appears to have returned to London for the rest of his days, and between 1636 and 1642 he published ten prose works, most of which are relatively short and can be described loosely as tracts or pamphlets. Peacham's early biographers have argued that, reduced to poverty in old age, he resorted to writing "penny pamphlets" in a desperate effort to obtain subsistence, but this view seems overromanticized, not to say unlikely.

I *Comical Fiction*: Coach and Sedan

Chronologically *Coach and Sedan, Pleasantly Disputing for Place and Precedence* (1636) was the first of the works that are the subject of this chapter. It is a delightful comic *tour de force* in dialogue form.[1] According to the dedication to Sir Elias Hicks, Peacham wrote the work at the request of his printer who did not wish to remain idle while Peacham completed another more serious piece (probably *The Truth of Our Times*). Earlier in the dedication Peacham excuses himself for writing "such light stuffe" (sig. A2^r) and, tongue-in-cheek no doubt, compares himself to Erasmus, Homer, and Sidney, all of whom, he claims, "sweetened their profoundest Studies, and greatest employments, with these and the like passages of inoffensive Mirth" (sig. A2^v). "I am no ordinary Pamphleter," he reminds the reader, "I would have thee to know; onely in Mirth I tried what I could doe upon a running subject, at the request of a friend in the *Strand*: whose leggs not so sound as his Iudgement, enforce him to keepe his Chamber, where hee can neither sleepe or studie for the clattering of *Coaches*" (sig. A3^r).

Peacham's "running" (i.e., topical) subject is chiefly concerned with the rival forms of transportation offered by the coach and the recently imported sedan chair. Other means of conveyance, such as

the Thames waterboat, the cart, and one's two legs are also discussed by various fictional characters who meet in a London street.
These same characters debate the controversial topic, concern for
which was elsewhere expressed in the "Proclamation for the Re-
straint of the Multitude and Promiscuous Uses of Coaches about
London and Westminster" (19 January 1635/36); the ballad entitled
The Coaches Ouerthrow, entered on the Stationer's Register ten
days after Peacham's work; and the pamphlet (now lost) entitled *The
Cart Accusing the Hackney Coach*, entered in the Register on 10
May that same year.[2]

As in the third part of *Graphice*, Peacham gives himself a central
role within the fictional framework of his sidewalk debate. Describing himself as "a peece of a Schollar" who has "seene the World
abroad in my travells, in many Countreys" and is now "returned to
make use (for the good of my selfe, and Countrey) of whatsoever I
formerly had knowne, or seene" (sig. B2^r), he breaks up a quarrel
between "a Gentleman of an auncient house" called Coach, and a
Monsieur Sedan. They are arguing over their respective superiority
and "which of them should deserue best of the commonwealth" (sig.
C2^v). The author-narrator is drawn into the debate as are various
passersby, among them Roger Dudgin (a carman), Powell (one of
Sedan's men), a country farmer, a Thames waterman, "an honest
plaine Countrey-Vicar" (once a fellow student of Peacham's at Cambridge),[3] and Beere-cart, who is called upon to make the final
judgment and reconcile the two principal parties in the debate.
Each man is made to speak in character, and much of the fun of
Coach and Sedan comes from Peacham's exploitation of the differ-
ences and antipathies of social classes underlying his representative
selection of English society. Coach, for example, boasts of his "many
quarter'd coates" of arms and of his acquaintance with every Lord
and Lady in the land (sig. B2^r). Monsieur Sedan boasts of his own
superiority with all the assurance of the new immigrant who
tactlessly insists on reminding the natives of all they owe to things
foreign (sig. B3^r). Roger Dudgin, who "comes whistling by with his
Carre, a lustie tall fellow red-hayr'd, and cheekes puffed and swolne
as if hee had beene a *Lincoln-shire-baggpipger*, or a *Dutch-
Trumpeter* under *Grobbendonck*, in a Canvas frocke, a red cap, a
payre of high-shooes, with his whip in his hand" (sig. B4^r), complains with all the self-righteousness of a working-class man about
the noise of coaches that causes poor apprentices to be "raysed vp
(before their houre) to their worke" (sig. B4^r). The waterman, proud

of his membership in an Ancient Company, talks ruefully about his financial difficulties due to the availability of hired coaches and sedan chairs (sig. C2^v).

Equally effective is Peacham's colorful representation of various aspects of English life, but principally that of London. We hear of Dol Turn-up and Peg Burn-it, "your silken wenches of *Hackney*" (sig. C1^r), who go to the Red-Bull and other playhouses; of citizen's wives who go to the London suburbs "under a colour of seeing their children at nurse to banquet with their sweet-hearts and companions" (sig. C1^v); and of the student in a school play who was "mervailously applauded," had apples tossed to him by maids, and was offered his schoolmaster's wife's bottle of Rosa-solis to drink (sig. C4^v). We hear of the Lord who would "leape out of his coach to play at stoole-ball with Country Wenches" (sig. D1^r), and of the Morris dance that happens to pass the disputants so that "away goes *Powell*, and takes the Maide-Marian, and the foole along to a Taverne" (sig. E2^r). Then—to conclude with two examples with familiar modern parallels—we learn of the noise of the ungodly who pass by the church in their coaches at sermon time (sig. E2^v), and of traffic congestion caused by coaches, so that whatsoever business a man has "hee must waite my Ladie (I know not whose) leasure (who is in the next shop, buying pendants for her eares: or a coller for her dogge) ere hee can find any passage" (sig. F1^r).

Obviously, fictional entertainment is Peacham's prime intent. He is not overly concerned with the very real contemporary problems posed by coaches which were hindering the flow of traffic in cities, threatening weak bridges in the country, churning up what highways there were, endangering pedestrians, creating a high volume of noise, and sapping the livelihood of those like the waterman who offered alternative forms of hired transportation. These matters are all mentioned by Peacham, but their manner of presentation is lightly humorous, and for a full sense of their seriousness we need to read the Royal Proclamations cited above. Presumably, however, like Bach's *Goldberg Variations*, Peacham's *Coach and Sedan* provided some relief for the suffering insomniac at whose instigation it had been composed.

II *Comical Fiction*: A Merry Discourse of Meum and Tuum

In 1639 Peacham again tried his hand at comic fiction in *A Merry Discourse of Meum and Tuum*. As before, he excuses himself for descending to "light exercises and mirthfull recreations" by citing

some worthy precedents, among them More's *Utopia* and Erasmus's
Praise of Folly. Abandoning the single-scene situation of *Coach and
Sedan*, he presents two comic rogues, Meum and Tuum, who set
out on a picaresque journey from their birthplace Wrangle (Lincs.)
to London and back.[4] Meum and Tuum come from a long line of
wranglers, amusingly listed as going back to the Tower of Babel and
Plutus's wife Eris. Twin sons of the usurer Harpax, Meum and
Tuum show their true character early in life: "they would seeme to
wrangle for the Mothers breast, and growne bigger, they would
scratch and take hold one of another" (p. 4). Not only do they never
agree, but, as they grow up, they shown an uncanny knack of creating dissension among others. Eventually they are forced out of the
village onto the highways of England, Peacham giving his fantasy
full play in his description of the clothes given them by their tight-
fisted father: "he clad each of them in a parchment suite, made of
old Bonds and Leases out of date; the large blacke lines served for
lace, and the waxen seales for buttons; for hats they had two old
Monmouth caps their father brought out of Wales, wherein they
stuck a Fen-Cats taile or two; weapons they had none, save each of
them a broom staffe in his hand, with some small summe of money
in their pockets" (pp. 5–6).

As they proceed south through East Anglia (Icenium), the towns
of Thetford (Sitomagum), Stow cum Quy (Qui), Cambridge, and
Trumpington, they leave a trail of havoc behind them. At one town,
for example, they make "worke a twelve Moneth after, for all the
Lawiers within tenne miles of that place" (p. 10). Their expertise in
legal chicanery improves as they practice their own version of
cony-catching activities: "we cut, nor picke no purses, [. . .] but
empty them after a legall way" (. 24).

As their journey unrolls, Peacham introduces a gallery of colorful
portraits, ranging from a Baker of Chesteron, who keeps count of his
drinks by undoing a succession of buttons, to a curate, who neither
preaches nor lives in his broken-down parsonage but "had a Flock-
bed upon a pallet in the Steeple of the Church, wch was both his
Chamber and his Study; the Presse wherein hee laid those books he
had, were holes in the walls, where Iack-Dawes had formerly bred;
neither did the Bells trouble his study, or his sleep, for they rang
not to prayers from one end of the weeke to another, except upon
the *Sunday,* and then not till ten a clock" (p. 7). In Cambridge
Meum and Tuum visit various places no doubt familiar to Peacham

from his undergraduate days, and they make a special point of learning all they can from "the Disputations, and wranglings of Sophisters" (p. 15). In London they familiarize themselves with the Courts of Law and have some painful adventures at the bear-baiting pit in Southwark. They then set out to return to Wrangle, on the way posing as fortune-teller and physician, "playing many merry trickes by the way" (p. 22).

Beneath the comic surface of Peacham's playful presentation there runs the constant moral that petty litigation and human dissension, often the result of acquisitiveness, are follies that are as ridiculous as they are universal. Possibly he had in mind the Chancery case in 1618 that split apart his own family, when his sister Anne took his father and brother to court over the matter of a deed to her first husband's estates,[5] but his choice of the names Meum and Tuum (Mine and Thine) clearly indicates that his fictional vision had more than personal implications and was intended, however gently, to lead the reader to self-examination.

III   *Essays:* The Truth of Our Times

In July, 1637, Peacham's "serious and laborious work" which he referred to in *Coach and Sedan* was entered on the Stationer's Register, but it was not printed until the following year. The sixty-year-old Peacham seems to have thought highly of *The Truth of Our Times: Revealed out of One Mans Experience, by Way of Essay,* and it seems to have taken him some time to complete. Perhaps this was because, as the title page hints, the work contains a summation of his life's experiences and something of a judgment upon the world as he saw it. In 1638, if we accept what Peacham says at face value, all his efforts over the years in education and in writing had gone largely unrewarded. His attempts to gain his just deserts had failed, he had suffered humiliation at the hands of the wealthy who have no regard for art or scholarship, and he had suffered the cultural starvation of one forced to teach "where scarce a gentleman, or any of civill carriage lived" (p. 123). Now he has given up "those vanities" of poetry, painting, music, and the mathematical sciences (p. 41), along with the thankless task of teaching (p. 26), and he is "exercised in another Calling" (p. 41)—except for pamphlet writing, one he does not reveal. He sees the world as increasingly enfeebled (p. 189), and engulfed in "vulgar ignorance and simplicity," which he blames upon "cunning Sectaries" (p. 183). It is "a cunning age" in which "if among one hundred of your acquaintance, yea five hundred, you meet with two or three faithfull friends, think your selfe happy" (p. 84).

To think of Peacham as embittered in his last years would, I think, be quite wrong, but certainly there is in *The Truth of Our Times* a vein of regret at unfulfilled ambitions mixed with the familiar belief of the elderly of all ages that the world has declined, a belief which in this instance matches the deep-seated expectation among Peacham's contemporaries at the turn of the century that the world was in fact close to its end. The more somber notes discernible in the general tone of *The Truth of Our Times* are in considerable contrast to the fun of *Meum and Tuum* or *Coach and Sedan*, but they point the way to Peacham's final writings—works which become overtly political in their protest against those forces that are threatening to destroy what was left of the world Peacham knew as a young man. *The Truth of Our Times*, however, has another prominent side, for in this book Peacham's wit, aided by some of his most polished prose, is at its most vigorous as he sets down a large part of his life's experiences as scholar, teacher, writer, traveller, and observer of men. The impression of Peacham we take away from this book is not in fact that of some crushed and embittered melancholic, but of a man who in spite of circumstances retained his humor, his sense of moderation, and an uncommon zest for life as he found it. Thus we find that Peacham's taste for the humorous anecdote is unabated, and his gift for conveying the vitality and color of the world he observed around him in city and country is everywhere apparent. Furthermore, as Robert Cawley has observed, "Stylistically, this is probably the best book he ever wrote in prose; scarcely a page exists that does not have an example of some figure revealing a mind that has trained itself to observe closely with perceptive awareness."[6]

Consisting of fourteen varied essays, *The Truth of Our Times* is Peacham's one contribution to the newly developed genre of the essay that came into prominence in England in the early seventeenth century. As it had been developed by Montaigne and others, the essay tended to be concerned with the expression of a personal point of view although in Peacham's case the primary object is always the enlightenment of others rather than the matter of mere self-expression. In this respect he follows in the footsteps of Francis Bacon, the man principally responsible for establishing the genre in

England. Both Montaigne and Bacon shared in the growing reaction among writers of their day against the florid and rotund oratorical period of the Ciceronian style of prose, and, repeating the prose revolution that had taken place in imperial Rome, they attempted a more concise, concrete, and direct style modelled upon Seneca and Tacitus. In Montaigne there is an accompanying tendency towards semi-colloquialism, so natural to his egoistic concern with his individual experiences and opinions. By contrast Bacon is far less familiar. His attitudes and style are more those of the objective analyst reflecting upon a variety of topics, all of which in the final version of his *Essayes Or Covnsels, Civill and Morall* (1625) tend to contribute, whatever their ostensible subject-matter, to an austere vision of life evaluated in terms of the tangibles of material and political success and failure.

Bacon's essays were very popular, and Peacham must have had them in mind when working on his own. Like Bacon, he has essays on friendship, parenthood, travel, and health, but he is no slavish imitator. Less austere than Bacon, his tone is more familiar and his style more discursive, but he shares with Bacon a concern for the good of the commonwealth, and his didactic goals are closer to those of Bacon than those of Montaigne. Typically Peacham, like other essayists of the time deals with a mixture of abstract and concrete subjects. Among the first category are his essays "Of Gods Providence," "Of Liberty," "Of Opinion," and "Of Discretion." More concrete are his discussions of such topics as "Of Schooles and Masters," "Of Making and Publishing Bookes," and "Of Parents and Children." One section entitled "A Religious Honest Man" is, however, less an essay than a "Character," another emerging seventeenth-century literary genre with which we now associate the names of John Earle and Sir Thomas Overbury.

When we read the essays, we discover that little has changed since Peacham wrote of similar matters in *The Compleat Gentleman.* He still believes that "There is no profession more necessary to the erecting the frame of a famous Common-wealth, than that of *Schoole-masters,* yet none in more dis-esteeme among the common vulgar, yea, and illiterate great ones" (p. 14). Schoolmasters still tend to be ignorant and parents indulgent. The granting of preferments still appears to have little connection with desert, and learning generally brings no certain promise of advancement (pp. 15–23). The writing of books "will hardly by a tenth part countervaile thy labour and charge" (p. 32), and the promises of the great are as empty as ever (p. 85). The English are still extravagant and too modish in their dress. Friendship is still a crucial matter requiring great care. About travel he is as enthusiastic as ever, believing that "The true taste of our lives sweetnesse is in travaile upon the way, at home, or abroad in other Countries" (p. 127).

These varied contents are framed by two essays that in some ways provide statements of what must have been the guiding principles of Peacham's experience. His opening essay concerns divine providence which, he announces, "from a childe I have seriously considered" (p. 1). God's protection, he maintains, is never denied those "who in singlenesse of heart have sought, and sincerely served him all their lives" (p. 2), and later, becoming very personal, he cites himself as a prime example of the Psalmist's belief that "When my Father and Mother forsooke me, thou oh Lord tookest me up" (p. 13), and he mentions how at a young age he was left to seek his fortune in the world but was attended by the providence of God "both at home, and abroad in other Countries, for which I had rather bee silently thankfull, than to proclaime the particularities; (which to some may seeme to bee fabulous and incredible) and for any thing I know, I and mine must say yet, (though in a farre different condition) with that Noble and great Earl of *Ireland*, *Gods Providence is our inheritance*" (pp. 13–14).

By contrast, his concluding essay, "Of Quietnesse and Health," may seem initially somewhat mundane. It talks of how "men now, for the most part, are not halfe so strong & vigorous as they were in the memory of our fathers" (p. 189), and cites the "arrowes of a yard or an ell long, which hang by the wals in many places of the North and west," the decrease in length of the shooting butts (mounds for archery practice) in country towns since the early part of Elizabeth's reign, and the changes in pikes and muskets "because our lesser bodies finde them rather for burthen than use" (p. 191). The cause Peacham partly attributes to "the world declining, and like a mother in her age, to bring forth but weake and shortlived children" (p. 191), but man himself is also partly responsible through excess of diet, lack of exercise, luxury, and incontinence. The real theme of Peacham's final essay emerges when we find him, as so often in his writings, urging the virtue of temperance. Though he also stresses the benefits of good health (itself a product of temperance), liberty, and tranquility of mind, all comes down ultimately to this one cen-

tral virtue, and his closing words are: "that wee may live to serve
God, to doe our King and Country service, to bee a comfort to our
friends, and helpfull to our Children, and others that depend upon
us, let us follow Sobriety and Temperance, and have (as *Tully* saith)
a diligent care of our health, which we shall bee sure to doe, if we
will observe and keepe that one short (but true) rule of *Hippocritas,
All things moderately, and in measure*" (p. 203).

IV   *"Rare Passages"*: The Valley of Varietie

Entered in the Stationer's Register in March, 1638, *The Valley of
Varietie* was described on its title page as a "Discourse fitting for the
Times, Containing very Learned and rare Passages out of Antiquity,
Philosophy, and History." As this implies, and as his dedicatory
epistle to Henry, Earl of Dover, makes clear, Peacham's work is a
series of selected rarities culled from the writings of others and
collected together "to enable Ingenious and Schollerly Discourse"
(sig. A4^r). His epistle to the reader further explains that what follows
"are *Collections* which I have at leasurable houres, collected out of
Pancirolla and other Authors." Apparently Peacham had intended
to translate Guido Pancirolli's *Rerum Memorabilium Sive Deper-
ditarum* (1599) into English, but, as he says, "having little leasure,
and expecting lesse gaine for so great a labour, in these unthankfull
times; wherein to be ignorant, is accounted by too many, to be a
Gentleman-like Qualitie. I resolved to give the world a taste of the
Fruit, before I opened the Basket" (sig. A5^{r-v}).[7]

Pancirolli's work is a compendium of exempla, anecdotes, and
information about the ideas, beliefs, artifacts, and institutions of the
ancients. As such it may be classed with much of that vast Renaissance literature of vulgarization designed to disseminate the moral,
philosophic, and scientific ideas of the ancients among ordinary men
of the time. Such "Storehouses," "Remaines," and "Treasuries"
were very popular and they frequently provide printed equivalents
for that typical Renaissance document, the commonplace book, in
which a man would customarily jot down notes and quotations from
anything in his reading that interested him. Pancirolli's book has
little of the haphazard format of a typical commonplace book, however, for he carefully selects and arranges his material into two
categories, the first dealing with commodities and institutions
known in the ancient world and lost to the modern, and the second
(significantly much shorter) dealing with modern inventions. Of the

eight chapters that Peacham takes from Pancirolli, seven are from
his first category: "Of that Fire which perpetually burneth in ancient
Monuments," "Of the ancient Triumphs among the Romanes," "Of
Cinnamome," "Of Balsamum," "Of incombustible Flaxe, or which
will not consume by Fire," "Of an artificiall kinde of guilding
amongst the Romanes, which they called *Pyropus,* as also of *Elec-
trum,*" and "Of Glasse made Malleable, to be beaten forth every
way." Only the chapter "Of Bells," which is claimed as a Christian
invention, is taken from Pancirolli's second category.

Peacham does not follow Pancirolli's two-part system, although
most of his other chapters are quite in keeping with those he has
culled from his Italian model. It seems probable, as Peacham's epistle to the reader states, that all of his chapters are from some secondary source or other.[8] Chapter One ("What to thinke of the length of
Age, Men lived in former Times, and shortly after the Creation")
and Chapter Twenty ("A most ancient and pleasant manner of
Choosing their Prince in *Carinthia*") seem to be based respectively
on passages in Thomas Milles's *The Treasurie of Auncient and Moderne Times* (1613) and *Times Store-House* (1619), themselves both
translations of all manner of quotations from various European writers, but the multitude of such borrowings during the period may
mean that some further intermediary source is involved. Nonetheless, the personality of Peacham is not totally obscured. "Of *Margaret* the Wife of *Herman,* Earle of *Henneberge,*" for example, is a
chapter of his own, in which he tells the story of the unfortunate
countess who "being about forty yeares of age, upon Easter day, and
about nine of the clocke in the yeare of our Lord, 1276, was brought
to bed of three hundred and sixtie and five children, all which were
baptized in two brazen Basons, by *Guido* the Suffragane of *Vtrecht*"
(p. 142). Peacham insists that "I my self have twice or thrice, when I
lived in *Holland,* seen" the marble epitaph that recounts this story,
and this same stress upon his own experience is matched in his
chapter on incombustible flax or Asbestinum where he inserts into
his translation from Pancirolli a typically personal anecdote: "Yet I
remember I had given me by an *Arabian,* when I lived in Saint
Martins Parish in the Fields, twentie yeares since, a pretty quantity
of a Stuffe like Flaxe, which he bad mee put into the fire, but it
consumed not" (pp. 130–31). However, such delightful intrusions
by the author are rare in the work and do little to relieve its tedium.
Even where Peacham is writing on a topic familiar and important to

him, as in the chapter on "What Studies and Exercises best become Princes," he seems unable to lift his material above the merely mundane. The stamp of Peacham's lively wit and irrepressible habit of personal digression thus barely makes itself felt, but in fairness one should add that the presumed attractions that Peacham's collection may well have had for his contemporaries are not usually shared by the twentieth-century reader.

V   *Cautionary Advice:* The Worth of a Peny

Like many of his contemporaries, Peacham had always placed a high value on the virtue of thrift, and it comes as no surprise to find him completing at the age of sixty-three an entire work on the subject. Entitled *The Worth of a Peny: Or, A Caution to Keep Money*, the book was entered in the Stationer's Register on 20 April, 1641, and printed the same year by Richard Hearne. There is a possibly unique copy of this edition in the Huntington Library. More common are copies published without the printer's name and dated 1647. These are made up from the same sheets as the 1641 impression, only the title page being changed. Doubtless Peacham would have been surprised to learn that *The Worth of a Peny*, which he dedicated to Richard Gipps, turned out to be his most popular work.[9] During the seventeenth century alone ten editions were printed with more to follow in the eighteenth and nineteenth centuries.

Although the book is primarily an exhortation to thrift, it also attempts to analyze the social and economic causes of poverty and to suggest to the reader how poverty may be avoided. Peacham argues that the principal causes of contemporary poverty are related to the acquisition of vast wealth by only a few men, who, unlike their feudal predecessors, "so brood over, and watch it day and night, that it is impossible for Charity to be regarded, Vertue rewarded, or Necessitie relieved" (sig. A3^v). Remarks on the harmful effects of removing money from circulation lead Peacham to reiterate the commonplace view of his age, derived from Aristotle, that prodigality is preferable to covetousness, since the prodigal man at the very least benefits "every trade and vocation," especially "the Tailor, Haberdasher, Vintner, Shoemakers, Sempsters, Hostlers, and the like" (sig. A4^r). He then argues that peace has partly caused the current problem since vanity and idleness now thrive, that foreigners are exploiting Britain (sig. A4^v), that trade in England has declined, that rents have risen, and that "Scholars without money get neither Patrones nor preferment, Mechanique Artists no work, and the like of other professions" (sig. B1ʳ).

Peacham also admits that there coexist the age-old universal causes of poverty among individuals, such as extravagance, falling victim to fraud, idleness, marriage "for a little handsomnes and eie-pleasing beautie" rather than for a sound economic alliance, accidents of fire or robbery, and sickness. In addition, some men by their very station in life are necessarily poor, since "There must, by Divine *Providence*, in the body of a Common-wealth, be as well poore as rich" (sig. B3ʳ). After grim talk about the miseries of want and an amusing digression upon what a penny can buy, Peacham concludes with some advice on thrift. His theme is moderation, and he urges his readers to take the Aristotelian middle road between covetousness and prodigality, particularly in matters of diet, dress, and recreation. Anyone facing hardship should consider what trade or profession he was brought up to, and, if none, what his "Genius, or naturall disposition standes most affected unto" (sig. E3ʳ). Military service in the Netherlands or emigration to the New World are both recommended as financially beneficial.

The social or economic historian will find this summary commonplace, even trite, but the student of literature will be struck by certain other features not already mentioned. Like a good many of his fellow writers who wrote didactic and cautionary works, Peacham enlivens his work with anecdotal examples. A number of these are very humorous and show him indulging to his advantage in what, as we have already seen, was a favorite technique and one that he excelled in. Typical is his story of some Cambridge students:

A peny may save the credit of many, as it did of foure or five young Scholers of Cambridge, who going into the Towne to break their fast with puddings (having sent to their Colledge for bread and beere) the Hostesse brought them twelve puddings broil'd, and finding among themselves that they had but eleven pence, they were much troubled about the other peny, they neither having any book about them to lay pawn for it: quoth one, bolder then the rest, *Audaces Fortuna juvat;* Fortune favours the venturous, and biting off a piece of the puddings end, by wonderfull luck spite out a single peny that paid for it, which it seemes was buried in the oat-meale, or spice, so for that time they waved their credits. (sig. D1ᵛ)

Throughout Peacham also inserts a succession of personal anecdotes, particularly when recounting his experiences in the Netherlands, in Lincolnshire, or in London:

I remember when I was in the Low Countries, there were three souldiers, a
Dutchman, a Scot, and an Englishman, for their misdemeanors condemned
to be hanged: yet their lives were begd by three severall men, one a
Bricklayer, that he might help him to make bricks & carry them to walls,
the other was a Brewer of Delft, who beg'd his man to fetch water and do
other worke in the Brewhouse; now the third was a Gardiner, and desired
the third man to help him to worke in, and to dresse an Hop-garden: the
first two accepted their offers thankfully, this last the Englishman told his
maister in plaine termes his friends never brought him up to gather Hops,
but desired he might be hang'd first, and so he was. (sig. B3^v)

The enjoyment of this book owes much to the sprightly style with
which Peacham recounts such anecdotes, and his skillful weaving of
them into the fabric of what could otherwise have been a dull
thirty-five page lesson on a well-worn topic. Doubtless his seventeenth-century readers felt the same attraction and relished the
manner in which "serious" reading could in his hands be a vehicle
for fun.

VI *Cautionary Advice:* The Art of Living in London

Like many of his contemporaries Peacham was aware of the dangers that lie in wait for anyone who comes to the city unused to its
ways, and it is this thought that apparently prompted him in 1642 to
write an eight-page pamphlet: *The Art of Living in London, or, A
Caution how Gentlemen, Countreymen and Strangers, drawn by
occasion of businesse should dispose of themselves in the thriftiest
way, not onely in the Citie, but in all other populous places.* As in
The Worth of a Peny, Peacham adopts his favorite role of teacher-
guide and once again offers practical advice on personal conduct and
in particular on thrift. The city, he says, "is like a quick-sand, the
longer you stand upon it, the deeper you sinke; if here, mony or
meanes to get it be wanting" (sig. A2^r). Its distractions are many, "as
perpetuall visits of vaine and uselesse acquaintance; necessitous
persons ever upon borrowing hand with you; cloathes in the fashion,
this or that new Play, play at Ordinaries, Taverne feasts and meet-
ings, Horse and Coach hire; besides those britle comodities they

carry; Boat-hire to *Kingston, Windsor,* and other places, with the like" (sig. A2^r). Corrupt grooms and laundresses, prostitutes, and pickpockets are everywhere, and these last are so clever that Peacham cannot resist a brief anecdote to illustrate their activities. A tradesman's wife, returning from a play, discovered that her purse was gone. "Quoth her husband, where did you put it? Vnder my Peticote, between that and my smocke. What, quoth he, did you feele no bodies hand there? Yes, quoth shee, I felt ones hand there; but I did not thinke hee had come for that" (sig. A4^r).

Such descriptions of the tricks that may be played upon the unwary suggest that we should categorize this pamphlet with that vast body of sixteenth- and seventeenth-century literature concerned with the activities of "cony-catchers" or what we would call "con men." Much of this literature was ostensibly didactic in intent, but clearly more often than not its high-sounding moral guidance was just an excuse to sanction witty, humorous, and often bawdy accounts of criminal behavior. In many instances the plea of *utile et dulce* was stretched very thin, but in the case of *The Art of Living in London,* the entertaining anecdotes never get out of hand, and a very sizeable proportion of the pamphlet does indeed consist of well-intentioned practical advice. The newcomer, for example, is urged to lodge "in some honest house of credit" (sig. A2^r), he should finish his business as expeditiously as possible, at all cost avoid idleness, surround himself with books of piety, look after his horse himself, avoid running up credit, have food sent to his chamber, using the leftovers for breakfast the next morning, and keep out of crowds where pickpockets thrive. The inexperienced visitor to New York, Rome, or London might well find much to ponder here.

As must be obvious, Peacham was familiar with the literature of roguery that had proved so popular ever since Gilbert Walker, John Awdeley, and Thomas Harman in the mid sixteenth century began writing about the Elizabethan underworld, the criminals who peopled it, and the tricks and deceptions by which they thrived. With Robert Greene's *A Notable Discovery of Cozenage* (1591) the genre became fully established and was to flourish throughout the early years of the seventeenth century. Peacham's anecdotes concerning criminal behavior, both in *The Art of Living in London* and in certain of his other writings such as *Meum and Tuum,* are typical of the genre and in their manner of presentation owe much to such precursors as Harman and Greene. Where Greene, however, tended increasingly to sympathize with his rogue anti-heroes, often in contradiction to his expressed moral purposes, Peacham, as already implied, retains a careful balance between entertainment and didacticism.

Among the writers of such literature imitation and at times outright plagiarism of each other's works were common, and Peacham was clearly no exception regarding his indebtedness to other writers. At one point in *The Art of Living in London*, for example, he gives a shortened version of the common roguish trick described by Greene at the opening of his *A Notable Discovery* and his final sentence may even indirectly allude to his source:

Againe, walking abroad, take heed with what company you sort your selfe withall: if you are a countrey man, and but newly come to towne, you will be smelt out by some cheaters or other, who will salute, call you by your name (which perhaps one of their company meeting you in another street, hath learned by way of mistaking you for another man, which is an old tricke) carry you to the Taverne, saying they are a kin to some one dwelling neere you, &c. But all trickes of late yeares have been so plainly discovered, and are so generally knowne almost to every childe, that their practice is out of date and now no great feare of them; yet an Item can doe you no hurt.
[Sig. A4^r]

In moral outlook Peacham and Greene may have had little in common, but in his use of the lively anecdote Peacham appears to have learned much from his notorious contemporary.

VII *Polemic:* The Duty of All True Subiects

The final group of four works to be considered in this study all show how Peacham, a man of moderate Royalist and Anglican sympathies, became caught up between 1639 and 1642 in that great stirring of contentious forces which within a short time was to lead to civil war, the establishment of the Commonwealth, and the execution of Charles I. The first work belonging to this group is *The Duty of All True Subiects to their King*,[10] which Peacham dedicated to the wealthy and powerful Royalist, Sir Paul Pindar. Pindar had on occasion made enormous loans to the King—a matter to which Peacham indirectly alludes (sig. *1^v)—and Peacham obviously feels confident that his dedicatee is an ideal model for those who wish to serve their king and country and provide for "the advancement of Gods Church and true Religion" (sig. *2^r). From the beginning Peacham strikes

the note of concern that is to vibrate through each of his polemical
works. He talks of the "hard and dangerous times" (sig. *1ᵛ) and
refers directly to "these tumults and commotions, that of late
yeares, and daily doe arise" (sig. *4ʳ), their cause, as he sees it,
proceeding "from a pretence of *conscience,* and *Reformation of
abuses in the Church,* under which colour our obstinate Innovators
bandie themselves against their owne good and Religious Kings"
and "against our Reverend Bishops." Of would-be reformers he
adds that "We need neither them nor their reformation, our Church
of England, being as well setled and governed as any in the Christian world" (sig. *4ʳ). Peacham's loyalties with regard to contemporary debate over the monarchy and proposed reformation of the
established Church (particularly in the matter of episcopacy) are
thus made clear from the outset.

The text of his tract is divided into two parts, corresponding to the
two central points of his argument. The first part concerns the duty
and loyalty which, he believes, every subject owes to his king; the
second part concentrates upon the love and duty owed to one's
country. Peacham's method is the familiar listing of biblical, historical, and legendary exempla in support of his thesis, but for obvious
reasons there is an urgency about his writing not present in earlier
works, particularly at the opening and close of the pamphlet. At the
outset, for example, there is a striking piece of prose, some of which
was quoted above in Chapter 2, comparing the King to Orpheus
(sig. A2ʳ), and at the conclusion there is a plea, significantly echoing
part of the Anglican liturgy, for peace in our time: "Let us therefore
be warned, and earnestly entreate of the Lord of Hosts, that hee
would give unto us understanding hearts, able hands, peace in these
our dayes, unanimity in our resolutions, and constancy in our loves,
and loyalty to our most dread Soveraigne King *Charles,* and to our
deare nursing mother, this famous and most flourishing Country of
England" (p. 63). Yet, like those who made similar pleas in the
Europe of the 1930s, Peacham was to see his worst fears confirmed
within a few years.

VIII   *Polemic:* A Dialogue between the Crosse in Cheap, and Charing Crosse

Between 1639 and 1641, this last being the date of Peacham's *A
Dialogue between the Crosse in Cheap, and Charing Crosse,*[11] the
English had witnessed the failure of Charles I in the two "Bishops

Wars" to impose a Book of Common Prayer and a return to episcopacy in Scotland, and they had seen the election of the "Long Parliament" and the subsequent beginnings of a radical shift of power
from royal prerogative to constitutional monarchy and vigorous
moves toward the abolition of episcopacy and the traditional structure of Anglican church government. Archbishops Laud and Williams together with various other bishops had been confined to the
Tower, while several Puritan agitators had been released from jail to
popular acclaim. To any Conformist or Royalist such events seemed
dire threats to the entire body politic of the realm, and not surprisingly the tension between Puritans and Parliamentarians on the one
hand, and Conformists and Royalists on the other, increased
dramatically. It was soon obvious to many that civil conflict was
imminent.

An odd side issue that developed early in 1641 was the attention
focused upon the ancient stone cross in Cheapside, a familiar London landmark first erected by Edward I in 1289 and restored by
Queen Elizabeth in 1600. For Puritans the monument was an
idolatrous and symbolic image of the "popish" tendencies which
they felt were prominent in the Anglican church. Several pamphlets
were published setting out this view, among them George Abbot's
Cheap-side Crosse Censured and Condemned (1641) and the
anonymous *The Pope's Proclamation* (1641).[12] In answering pamphlets the Conformists condemned the Puritans for extremism,[13]
while tactfully not forgetting to condemn the Papists also.

Peacham's brief four-leaf contribution to the pamphlet war is a
dialogue in which the two sister crosses of Cheapside and Charing
discuss their precarious existence in "these uncertaine times." A
woodcut on the title page vividly portrays their situation. To the left
is Charing Cross, already long fallen into decay and minus its cross.
It is supported by two square-capped bishops. One says, "Help
Wren, or we are undone men," and the other replies, "It shall not
fall, To ruine all." To the right is Cheapside Cross, just as she
describes herself in the text: "marvellously beautified and adorned
[. . .] and fenced about with sharp pointed barres of Iron, against
the rude and villanous hands of such as upon conditions as they
might have the pulling of mee downe" (sig. A3^r).[14] An Anabaptist to
her left declares: "O Idoll now, downe must thou," and a Brownist,
who has scaled the railings, answers: "Brother Ball be sure it shall."
The dialogue between the two crosses is an amusing fantasy which

recounts the history of crosses and makes fun of the irrational extremism of those who wish to demolish Cheapside Cross (Charing Cross presumably being so far decayed that she is not considered a problem). Cheap asks why those who accuse her of being a Papist do not ask the King to file off the cross on the royal crown, and she recounts the story of the woman who this last week "beat her maid pittifully for laying (as shee made her masters bed) by chance, two bed-staves a crosse" (sig. A3ᵛ). The obvious point made by such anecdotes is further underlined toward the end when Charing suggests that the cause of their current difficulties "is a distraction and giddines in profession of religion, that every one almost is led by his owne opinion" (sig. A4), a theme that Peacham takes up the following year in *Square-Caps Turned into Round-Heads*.

The voice of reason, however, went unheard, and on 24 January, 1642 an angry crowd attacked and defaced Cheapside Cross, which, "receiving a mortall wound, [. . .] and being past care," became "as dead as old *Charin Crosse* in the strand."[15] The event brought forth more pamphlets, and there was a call for the total destruction of the cross.[16] Eventually, late in April, 1643, Parliament confirmed an order of the London Council for the levelling of Cheapside Cross, and on 2 May, "amidst signes of public rejoicing," one of London's oldest and most splendid monuments was torn to the ground.[17] Peacham's reaction is not recorded but in keeping with the general tenor of his pamphlet he would no doubt have deplored the destruction as unnecessarily extremist.

IX   *Polemic:* A Paradox in the Praise of a Dunce, To Smectymnuus *and* Square-Caps Turned into Round-Heads

The title and date of Peacham's *A Paradox in the Praise of a Dunce* (1642), especially his addressing it "To Smectymnuus," suggest that Peacham was well aware of the theological pamphlet debate between Bishop Hall and "Smectymnuus." Joseph Hall, at the suggestion of Archbishop Laud, had published his *Episcopacie by Divine Right Asserted* in February, 1640, and this defense of the Anglican episcopacy set off a long and acrimonious controversy. Before it concluded, it tempted the pen of John Milton, a matter familiar to literary students, but, as will be seen, it also drew two responses from Peacham, something that has generally not been recognized in accounts of the affair.[18]

Among scholars there is general agreement concerning the main outlines of the pamphlet war. In January, 1641 Hall followed up his first pamphlet with *An Humble Remonstrance to the High Court of Parliament*, and in March this was attacked in *An Answer to a Book Entitled an Humble Remonstrance* by "Smectymnuus," a name composed of the initials of the five Puritan divines who had composed it. Attached was an anonymous *Postscript* commenting on the history of the episcopacy, now generally believed to be by Milton. Hall replied to Smectymnuus in April with *A Defence of the Humble Remonstrance*. This in turn drew a reply from Smectymnuus in *A Vindication of the Answer to the Humble Remonstrance* (June 1641) and a much fiercer attack by Milton, still writing anonymously, in *Animadversions upon the Remonstrants Defense against Smectymnuus*.[19] Hall then wrote *A Short Answer to the Tedious Vindication of Smectymnuus* (July 1641) and thereafter dropped out of the debate, but early in 1642 an anonymous supporter of Hall published *A Modest Confutation of a Slanderous and Scurrilous Libell, Entituled, Animadversions upon the Remonstrants Defense against Smectymnuus*, and shortly after in late winter or spring Milton replied in self-defense in *An Apology against a Pamphlet Call'd A Modest Confutation*. Where then do Peacham's two works fit into this complex sequence?

A Paradox in the Praise of a Dunce is impossible to attribute to any precise month. It is not entered in the Stationer's Register, and its text does not reveal any evidence that Peacham was responding to any specific passage in the pamphlets of either Smectymnuus or Milton. Indeed, but for the title, there is no real evidence in this pamphlet that Peacham had any desire to enter the fray at all, and his decision to address the work "To Smectymnuus" looks suspiciously like a commercial ploy designed to catch the eye of a potential buyer looking over a bookseller's wares. The four-leaf work is a paradoxical encomium, and its satire concentrates particularly on schoolmasters and churchmen, Anglicans and Puritans alike. Peacham's central point is that "as our Times are, the matter is not great whither a man be learned or a *Dunce*, for he may come to preferment as soone by the one as the other, though he were but a Tradesman, or a Mechanicke" (sig. A4^r). What he is implying in these concluding words is that the duncery of the established church, exemplified in the misuse of the preferment system, is in

134

part to blame for the chaotic situation that now prevails in the land. His own experience, as he points out at the beginning, demonstrates the Church's neglect of the very qualities it should most have valued:

But when I saw that I had spent no small a time in the Vniversity, published some usefull Bookes (as well in Latine as English) to the Commonwealth, which have taken in the world, and I could never get any thereby, but [. . .] silken words, I concluded I was no *Dunce* [. . .] had I bin *Dunce,* without question, I had long ere this, perhaps bin double or treble benefic'd, in a lasie Prebend, or Deane of some Cathedrall my selfe, or kept a fellowship with a good Living to boote in some Colledge or other, as long as I had lived. [sig. A3^r]

Satirical anecdotes about duncical churchmen and schoolmasters follow, and Conformist and Separatist churchmen alike are subject to Peacham's caustic wit.[20] It is an amusing work, and its surface tone is light and good-humored. However, the issues Peacham raises are serious enough, and the hint of personal bitterness with which the work opens provides the pamphlet with a complex but balanced point of view that is generally absent from most partisan pamphlets of the time. Indeed, the casual reader of *A Paradox* may be forgiven for not perceiving that Peacham's sympathies are with the Anglican cause.

Square-Caps Turned into Round-Heads by contrast leaves no such room for misinterpretation. Furthermore, it shows Peacham deliberately attempting to identify himself with Bishop Hall in the Smectymnuan debate. The chief matters of contention in the controversy concerned two issues: liturgy and church government. Hall espoused a vision of authority and order. In his eyes the Anglican liturgy had its roots in the practices of the ancient church and bishops received their power through apostolic authority. The Smectymnuans, however, were against a fixed liturgy. They believed in spontaneous prayer and proposed a church more democratically governed, contending that there were no convincing arguments in antiquity for the office of bishop. By 1642 events themselves were increasingly providing their own solution to the vital issues of the debate. The power of the bishops had dwindled in particular, and in February they were expelled from the House of Lords and deprived of all temporal authority.

Peacham's pamphlet, which is in dialogue form, presents two characters, Time and Opinion, who represent diametrically opposed views of those pro-episcopacy on the one hand, and the Puritans (or Roundheads) on the other. On the title page is an emblematic woodcut showing on the left Time with an inverted scythe and broken hourglass, and on the right Opinion, represented as a Puritan woman who turns a wheel at the top of which are effigies of Roundheads and at the bottom the square caps of five bishops. Below are some verses: "*Time* doth *Opinion* call unto accompt,/ Who turnes the *Bishops* downe and *Round-Heads* mount:/ Vpon Her lofty Wheele their Noddels are;/ But Her *Camelian* feedeth on His aire."[21] Time represents the conformist Anglican view and speaks throughout in vindication of the bishops. The argument goes entirely his way, and he concludes forcibly with a reminder to Opinion: "Well *Opinion, Omnia tempus habent*, and my comfort is this, *Nullum violentum diaturnum:* Nothing violent lasts long" (p. 8). For her part, Opinion is represented as a giddy creature, as changeable as her chameleon. Ultimately she admits: "I am carried, with violence in the throng I can doe no other than I doe" (p. 8). As the argument proceeds, there is never any doubt as to which side Peacham's sympathies are committed. As the title page states, he is concerned with "the worthinesse" of Time and "the folly" of Opinion. Like Time, he clearly desires "no *Innovation* either in *Church* or *Common-wealth*" (p. 3), and his attitude to Opinion is made clear when he has her admit (p. 2) to having been born at "Swine drecht" (Pig Muck).

Peacham's connection with the Smectymnuan controversy emerges on page six. In his "Postscript" Milton had given a series of histories of those English bishops who had led shameful lives. Among the various misdemeanors he described were Bishop Chichele's diversion of King Henry V "that was looking too neerely into the superfluous revenues of the Church, to a bloody warre," and the "intolerable pride, extortion, bribery, luxurie of *Wolsey*."[22] In his reply to Milton's "Postscript," Hall in *A Defense of the Humble Remonstrance* referred to Milton's contribution as a "rhapsody of histories" and a "tedious relation," and then said of Milton's accusations:

What! are these the only remarkable works that your eyes could discover to fall from the hands of bishops? Could you see no colleges, no hospitals built?

no churches re-edified? no learned volumes written? no heresies confuted?
no seduced persons reclaimed? no hospitality kept? no great offenders
punished? no disorders corrected? no good offices done for the public? no
care of the peace of the church? no diligence in preaching? no holiness in
living?[23]

In *Animadversions* Milton quoted and answered all but two of the
above questions in a scathingly negative riposte.

Then, either in response to Milton or independently in his own
reaction to Hall, Peacham replied to certain of Hall's questions as
positively as he was able. Time begins by paraphrasing Hall and
asks: "Who have built more Colledges in our Famous *Vniversities*,
more Churches, Hospitalls &c. in any part of Europe, then our
Bishops have done in England?" Opinion then replies in a manner
reminiscent of Milton: "Did not your great *Gor-bellied Cardinall
Wolsey* pull down forty houses of Religion, to found His Colledge in
Oxford? which He left unfinished." But Time replies: "He had
finished it, if he had liv'd, and made it one of the fairest Colledges of
the world. But since you speak of Oxford and him, let me tell you
what *Bishops* have done in *Oxford* and *Cambridge*" (p. 6).

This is the cue for Peacham to show the fruits of his historical
knowledge in a list of bishops who founded colleges at the two
universities, and he repeats the story he had already told elsewhere
of Henry Chichele (significantly one of the bishops attacked by Milton in his "Postscript"), a man of humble origins who eventually
became Archbishop of Canterbury. From universities Peacham
shifts to schools and, with Hall's list of questions in mind, he gives
special place to John Williams, made Archbishop of York the previous November by Charles I. Peacham recounts how Williams
beautified the Church of Westminster when he was Dean there,
how when Bishop of Lincoln he repaired the palace and purchased
books for the library, how he endowed a school and hospital in
Wales, and how he set up annuities for the poor and scholarships for
students at Westminster and St. John's, Cambridge.[24] Peacham's
warm praise of Williams was something of a brave challenge in 1642.

Williams's appointment as Archbishop had roused the intense ire
of the Commons which had been further compounded when, after a
hostile mob prevented his entering Parliament in December, 1641,
he and other bishops had signed a petition to the King urging that
because of their enforced absence the proceedings of Parliament in

the interim should be considered null and void. As a result the Archbishop was not surprisingly imprisoned on 30 December. This, however, had done little to cool the popular dislike of him which continued to be vented in such pamphlets as *Three Looks Over Lincoln* (?January 1642), *The Decoy Duck* (January 1642), and L.P.'s *A New Disputation Between the Two Lordly Bishops, York and Canterbury* (February 1642). Peacham in *Square-Caps* thus abandons the good-humored fence-sitting that characterized *A Paradox* and firmly sides with the Anglican and Royalist cause. With armed conflict imminent he apparently also gives up his hope for some early victory of common sense and reason and instead places his faith in the power of Time to put all to rights. But, as we now know, it was some eighteen years before that restoration occurred.

CHAPTER 6

Conclusion

AFTER making his last statement on the vital religious and political issues of the day, Peacham perhaps left London to follow his king as so many of his persuasion did. Perhaps 1642 was indeed the year of his death, as most previous biographers have suggested. Or perhaps he went into seclusion to wait out events, only to die before any resolution of the conflict was in sight. All we know is that from 1642, apart from the poem attached to the 1644 Hollar engraving, the voice of Peacham is heard no more. Doubtless he would have been pleased, had he lived, to know that his most important work was reissued at the Restoration and skillfully edited to pay tribute to the sacrifices of those Royalists who had remained faithful and had assisted in the overthrow of the Commonwealth and the reestablishment of the Anglican church.

As we have seen, Peacham's writings are extremely varied, but throughout them the point of view is consistently that of Peacham, the scholar-teacher, attempting to reinforce values and institutions which he and a good many of his contemporaries felt were in decline. Like the Humanist scholar-teachers of a century before him, Peacham believes passionately in the importance of education for those born or called to govern and lead in Church and state. Like the Humanists, his concept of what that education should be is a broad one, and like them he feels that educators deserve a higher status than society has customarily accorded them. His religious and political views, as we have seen, are in the main conservative and traditional but not so rigid that he is incapable of perceiving the weaknesses and follies of the current conduct of the established Church and political system. For long an advocate of tolerance and the middle way, only at the close of his life does Peacham lose faith in the power of common sense and reason to overcome those forces that are about to change the course of English history.

138

Peacham's achievements as a writer are mixed. As a Humanist, the chief characteristic of his writing is its imitation of earlier works and its frequent dependencies and derivations give to his canon a resonance echoing many writers before him—Erasmus and More, Elyot and Ascham, Sidney and Puttenham, Lomazzo, Ripa and Vasari, Spenser, Hilliard, and Greene. Clearly his was not a particularly original or innovative mind, and it is consequently no accident that in actuality his most celebrated work, *The Compleat Gentleman,* is, with certain notable exceptions, a vast storehouse for the accumulated traditions and opinions of his sixteenth-century predecessors. One should thus be cautious about making over-ambitions claims for Peacham since almost everything he did appears to have been imitated or copied, and it would not be too far from the truth to say that he spent most of his writing life as a picker-up of considered trifles. As I have tried to demonstrate, however, there are compensations for Peacham's lack of originality.

Because of his inability to live solely by the pen, Peacham apparently never attempted to develop further the strengths that begin fleetingly to emerge in his later poetry. His emblems, on the other hand, though not particularly memorable for their verses, are for other reasons of major importance in the history of English emblem literature. His prose works, for their part, are often remarkable for their display of Peacham's humor, his gift for anecdote and the telling phrase, and his lively handling of fictional dialogue. As we have seen, two prose works stand out for the modern reader—*The Compleat Gentleman* and *The Truth of Our Times.* Both for their style and for that humane vision so representative of what we tend to admire most in the Renaissance mind these works have an especially enduring quality. As I have tried to show, however, it would be unfortunate if our appreciation of these works occurred at the cost of our enjoyment of the humbler but effective qualities of, say, *Graphice, Coach and Sedan, Meum and Tuum,* or *The Worth of a Peny.*

Finally for those of us who may from time to time feel stifled or overconstricted by the seemingly increasing demand in our age for "specialists" and for "specialized knowledge," Peacham has the further attraction of offering us the distant spectacle of a mind and an age free from such constraints where all areas of knowledge remain open to the inquirer and indeed are seen as necessary to the fulfillment of the complete man.

Notes and References

Preface

1. The single most important study of Peacham is Margaret C. Pitman's unpublished M.A. thesis "Studies in the Works of Henry Peacham," London University, 1933.

2. Robert R. Cawley, *Henry Peacham: His Contribution to English Poetry* (University Park, Pa., 1971); F. J. Levy, "Henry Peacham and the Art of Drawing," *Journal of the Warburg and Courtauld Insititute*, 37 (1974), 174–90; and Harold P. Levitt, "The Political Writings of Henry Peacham," Diss. New York University, 1968.

3. *The Truth of Our Times* (1638), p. 57.

Chapter One

1. *Graphice*, sig. A2^v.

2. *The More the Merrier* (1608), Ep. 43.

3. *The Truth of Our Times* (1638), sigs. A5^{r-v}.

4. Ibid., pp. 52–53.

5. Ibid., p. 39.

6. Ibid., pp. 31–32.

7. Ibid., p. 19.

8. Ibid., p. 26.

9. Louis B. Wright, *Middle-Class Culture in Elizabethan England* (1935; rpt. Ithaca, New York: Cornell University Press, 1958), pp. 170–200. The deliberately entertaining manner of both *The Worth of a Peny* and *The Art of Living in London* also relates them to the highly popular cony-catching literature of the period.

10. *The Compleat Gentleman*, p. 107; *Coach and Sedan*, sig. E2^r; *The Truth of Our Times*, p. 103. For details concerning the biography of the elder Henry Peacham, see my "Henry Peacham, Author of *The Garden of Eloquence* (1577): A Biographical Note," *Notes and Queries*, New Series, 24 (1977), 503–07.

11. *Graphice*, sig. A3^r.

12. See his *Thalia's Banquet* (1620), Ep. 70.

13. *The Compleat Gentleman*, p. 107.

14. *Minerva Britanna*, p. 98.

15. *Graphice*, p. 157; *Minerva Britanna*, p. 65. Cf. *Thalia's Banquet*, Ep. 51.

16. Jeremy Collier, *An Ecclesiastical History of Great Britain* (London: William Straker, 1852), VII, 337.

17. *The Compleat Gentleman*, p. 107

18. The two passages are joined by two and a half lines not in any extant text. The drawing is among the Marquess of Bath's manuscripts at Longleat (Wiltshire): Harley Papers, Vol. 1, fol. 159^b. See E. K. Chambers, "The First Illustration to 'Shakespeare'," *The Library*, 4th Series, 5 (1925), 326–30, Plate XI; John Dover Wilson, "*Titus Andronicus* on the Stage in 1595," *Shakespeare Survey*, 1 (1948), 17–22; and Samuel Schoenbaum, *William Shakespeare: A Documentary Life* (Oxford, 1975), pp. 122–23.

19. Schoenbaum, *William Shakespeare*, p. 123.

20. In *Thalia's Banquet* Peacham complains that he had to leave Trinity earlier than he would have liked ("To think how rawlie was I torne from it" [Ep. 51].

21. Margaret C. Pitman, "Studies in the Works of Henry Peacham," M.A. London University, 1933, pp. 16–17.

22. *The Art of Drawing*, sigs. I44^v–K1^r. Cf. *Graphice*, p. 167.

23. *The Compleat Gentleman*, p. 102.

24. *The Truth of Our Times*, p. 13.

25. For a summary of the evidence concerning Peacham's post in Kimbolton, see my "A Biographical Note on Henry Peacham," *Notes and Queries*, New Series, 24 (1977), 216.

26. Ibid., 215.

27. The music is to be found in the British Library at the back of Peacham's second *Basilicon Doron* manuscript emblem book (MS Harleian 6855, Art. 13). The music is on different paper and has been cropped to the size of the emblem book and could, therefore, be earlier than the remainder of the manuscript which dates from shortly after October, 1604.

28. See Peacham's dedication to James I in *Basilicon Doron* (MS Harleian 6855, Art. 13).

29. MS Rawlinson, poetry 146.

30. MS Harleian 6855, Art. 13. Peacham's dedication addresses James as "King of Great Britain," something which dates the work from after 20 October, 1604 when James proclaimed that this title should supersede that of "King of England, Scotland, France and Ireland."

31. See Peacham's dedication to Sir Julius Caesar in *Emblemata Varia*, his fourth manuscript emblem book (Folger Shakespeare Library: MS V. b. 45): "Annus iam agitur decimus septimus . . . ex quo Regiae Mati: REGIVM illud DONVM, totum in Emblemata versum et picturis ad vivum delineatis obtulerim quem libellum a sua ma^{te}: benigniter acceptum, . . . "

32. *Graphice* (1612), p. 73; *The Compleat Gentleman*, pp. 163–64.

33. *Graphice*, p. 166.

34. In *Graphice* Peacham refers to Christopher Collard of St. Martin's-in-the-Fields as "my scholar, now of Magdalene College, Oxford" (pp. 172, 173). Collard matriculated at Magdalen Hall on 14 June, 1611, and Peacham, who was a close friend of his parents (*Minerva Britanna*, p. 92), must have taught him shortly before then.

35. British Library: MS Royal 12A LXVI. The manuscript is referred to in *Minerva Britanna* where Peacham reminds the Prince that two years previously he had presented him with a version of *Basilicon Doron*, its "pictures drawen and limned by mine owne hand in their liuely colours" (sig. A2^r).

36. Sir Charles Cornwallis, *The Life and Death of Henry Prince of Wales* (1641), p. 101.

37. *Graphice*, p. 25.

38. Thomas Birch, *The Life of Henry Prince of Wales* (1760), p. 44.

39. James Cleland, *Propaideia, or The Institution of a Young Noble Man*, p. 35.

40. Sir Charles Cornwalis, *A Discourse of the Most Illustrious Prince, Henry* (1641), sig. C1^r.

41. *A Collection of Ordinances and Regulations* (1790). Published by the Society of Antiquaries.

42. *Minerva Britanna*, p. 39.

43. British Library: MS Royal 16 E XXXVIII.

44. *The Compleat Gentleman*, p. 195; *A True Relation*, sig. A3^r.

45. *The Compleat Gentleman*, p. 195.

46. *Prince Henrie Revived*, sig. A2^r; *Minerva Britanna*, p. 14.

47. *A True Relation*, sig. A3^v.

48. The article on Peacham in the *Dictionary of National Biography* contains a number of inaccuracies, among which is the statement that he went to Wymondham upon leaving university, and that while abroad he acted as tutor to the three elder sons of the Earl of Arundel (XV, 578–79). The schoolhouse in Wymondham was a guild chapel prior to the Reformation. It is now used as a public library. During 1615 Peacham's name was mentioned in the treason trial of Edmond Peacham, who attempted to implicate his namesake. For a brief account of this notorious affair, see my introduction to the facsimile edition of Peacham's *Emblemata Varia* (Ilkley and London, 1976).

49. *The Compleat Gentleman*, sig. A3^r. A description of William Howard's first meeting with Bishop Harsnet and of their departure for Norwich is given by Inigo Jones in a letter to the Earl of Arundel (17 Aug., 1620) which is quoted in Mary F.S. Hervey's *The Life, Correspondence and Collections of Thomas Howard, Earl of Arundel* (Cambridge: Cambridge University Press, 1921), p. 169.

50. *The Compleat Gentleman*, sig. B2^r.

51. J.H.F.H.S., *Blickling Hall*, 3rd revision (London: National Trust, 1976), p. 8. *Minerva Britanna* also furnished designs for four devices (ca. 1620) used in a plasterwork ceiling at Essex House in Houndsditch (since destroyed), see Margaret Jourdain, *English Decorative Plasterwork of the Renaissance* (London: B. T. Batsworth, 1926), figs. 23–25.

52. *Emblemata Varia* (ca. 1621–22) is signed "E Schola Martiniana ad campos" and in *The Valley of Varietie* (1638) Peacham says that he "lived in Saint *Martins* Parish in the Fields, twentie yeares since" (p. 130).

53. sig. C2^v.

54. *The Compleat Gentleman*, p. 199.

55. Ibid., p. 162.

56. The additions are sigs. X5, Y4, and Y5. A copy in the British Library (16576) contains sheets with an earlier and much shorter version of the Sackville entry mixed with sheets giving the newer and much longer version.

57. J.P. Collier, without citing any authority, claimed that Peacham was "a retainer in the family of Lord Dorset" in his *A Bibliographical and Critical Account of the Rarest Books in the English Language* (London: Joseph Lilly, 1865), II, 139.

58. sigs. A3^{r-v}, B3^r.

59. See my "A Biographical Note on Henry Peacham," *Notes and Queries*, New Series, 24 (1977), 216.

60. *Thestylis Atrata* (1634), sig. A2^v.

61. See "A Biographical Note on Henry Peacham," 216–17.

62. In *Coach and Sedan* (1636) Peacham introduces himself as one of his own characters and points out that he has not been in London for more than a dozen years (sig. E2^r).

63. sig. A2^v.

64. Gustav Parthey, *Wenzel Hollar, Beschreibendes Verzeichniss seiner Kupferstiche* (Berlin: Nicolai, 1853), No. 527.

65. Ibid. Nos. 229, 480, 490, 977, 1036.

66. *The Duty of All True Subjects*, pp. 31, 33.

67. "Studies in Peacham" (M.A. thesis), pp. 4–5, 70–71.

68. See W.L.'s "An Advertisement To the Reader" in *The Worth of a Peny* (1664 edition), sig. F2^v.

69. Referring to "my Kinsman Mr. *Henry* Peckham," author of *The Compleat Gentleman*, Webb says, " . . . Had my fates been such, I had been as near unto him in place of abode as I am in my love and in blood" (p. 145). I have been unable to establish the nature of the blood-relationship between Webb and Peacham.

70. *The Truth of Our Times*, p. 41.

71. Pitman in her thesis discusses the matter (p. 42), and, though the source has little authority, it is worth noting that Edmond Peacham be-

lieved that Henry was "a divine." Cf. John Besly, "Malone's Own Notes in Copies of Peacham's Various Publications," *Notes and Queries*, 1st Series, 11 (1855), 218.

72. Guildhall Library: MS 10091/18, fol. 36ᵇ. For further details about this document, see my Introduction to the facsimile edition of Peacham's *Emblemata Varia* (London and Ilkley, 1976).

73. The discrepancy in age may be a clerical error; it was not uncommon for a copyist to mistake 8 for 0.

74. *A Potent Vindication for Book-Making*, sig. A1ᵛ; *The Most Vendible Books in England*, sigs. Y1ᵛ and 2Eʳ.

75. Andrew Clark, *The Life and Times of Anthony Wood* (Oxford: Oxford Historical Society, 1891), I, 477. Cf. II, 335.

Chapter Two

1. On the complexities of the term "emblem," see Rosemary Freeman, *English Emblem Books* (London, 1948), pp. 37–39; and Henri Stegemeier, "Problems in Emblem Literature," *Journal of English and Germanic Philology*, 45 (1946), 26–37.

2. Quoted in Henri Estienne's *The Art of Making Devices*, trans. Thomas Blount (1650 ed.), sig. C1ᵛ.

3. *Of the Advancement and Proficience of Learning* (Oxford, 1640), Bk. 5, ch. 5, p. 255; cf. *Minerva Britanna*, sig. A3ᵛ.

4. Alciati's book in various forms and expansions, often accompanied by lengthy commentaries, appeared in over ninety editions throughout Europe in the sixteenth century alone.

5. Freeman, *English Emblem Books*, pp. 47–52; E.N.S. Thompson, *Literary By Paths of the Renaissance* (New Haven, 1924), p. 63.

6. The English translation of Van der Noot's *A Theatre for Worldlings* (1569) has some claim to be considered the first printed English emblem book.

7. Significantly two English editions of impresas—Samuel Daniel's translation of Giovio entitled *The Worthy Tract of Paulus Iovius* (1585) and Abraham Fraunce's *Insignium, Armorum, Emblematum, Hieroglyphicorum, et Symbolorum* (1588)—contain no illustrations.

8. *Palladis Tamia*, fol. 285ᵛ.

9. *The Art of Drawing*, sig. A2ᵛ. Cf. Nicholas Hilliard's comments in his manuscript treatise on the "Arte of Limning" (ca. 1598–1603), quoted by John Pope–Hennessy in "Nicholas Hilliard and Mannerist Art Theory," *Journal of the Warburg and Courtland Institute*, 6 (1943), 92.

10. Admittedly there is no actual proof that Peacham did prepare his own blocks. On this matter, see the discussion by James Clarke in "Henry Peacham's *Minerva Britanna* (1612): A Bibliographical Description and Analysis," Diss. University of Leeds, 1977.

11. *Minerva Britanna*, sig. A3ʳ.

12. *The Compleat Gentleman*, p. 199.

13. *Thalia's Banquet*, Ep. 70.

14. Though the *Minerva Britanna* collection and most of his individual emblems used woodcut pictures, Peacham may have tried his hand at engraving for the unsigned emblems in *A True Relation* and *The Valley of Varietie*. He may also have engraved the portrait frontispiece to *Prince Henrie Revived* (1615). According to Horace Walpole, he engraved a portrait of Sir Thomas Cromwell after Holbein, see *Anecdotes of Painting in England*, ed. Ralph N. Wornum (London: Henry G. Bohn, 1849), III, 880.

15. For additional information concerning this manuscript, see my "Henry Peacham's First Emblem Book," *Bodleian Library Record* (forthcoming).

16. C. E. Wright, *Fontes Harleiani* (London: British Museum, 1972), p. 247.

17. *A Catalogue of the Harleian Manuscripts* (London: British Museum, 1808), II, 118.

18. C. E. Wright (ed.), *Diary of Humphrey Wanley* (London: Bibliographical Society, 1966), I, xx–xxi.

19. Arundell J. K. Esdaile, *The British Museum Library* (London: Allen and Unwin, 1946), p. 231. For further details concerning this manuscript, see my "Henry Peacham, Ben Jonson, and the Cult of Elizabeth-Oriana," *Music and Letters* (forthcoming).

20. Freeman, *English Emblem Books*, pp. 80–82.

21. *Minerva Britanna*, pp. 15, 20, 46, 47, 56, 58, 116, 128, 149, 166.

22. Cesare Ripa, *Iconologia* (Rome, 1603), p. 480. Unless otherwise stated, all references to Ripa will be to this edition.

23. Alfred E. Newton, *The Greatest Book in the World* (London: John Lane, 1926), p. 177.

24. *The Basilicon Doron of King James VI*, ed. James Craigie (Edinburgh and London: Scottish Text Society, 1944), II, 9.

25. On the various methods employed to order and unify the collections of other authors, see Thompson, *Literary By Paths*, pp. 46, 51, 53, 59–60.

26. Whitney makes the theoretical distinction in his preface but makes no attempt to divide his book along these lines.

27. Bk. III, Ch. 10, 1118a. Cf. Spenser, *Faerie Queene*, I.iv.21; John Davies of Hereford, *Humours Heav'n on Earth* (1605), st. 16.

28. *Iconologia* (Rome, 1593), p. 111. Whether Peacham knew Ripa's work in 1604 is difficult to determine. His contemporary, Ben Jonson, was using an edition by early 1604 (see Allan H. Gilbert, *The Symbolic Persons in the Masques of Ben Jonson* [Durham, N. Carolina, 1948], p. 4), and Peacham certainly had a copy by his side when he prepared *Minerva Britanna* (see Freeman, *English Emblem Books*, pp. 79–81).

29. Mario Praz, *Studies in Seventeenth-Century Imagery*, 2nd ed. (Rome: Edizioni di Storia e Letteratura, 1964), p. 58. Cf. Robert Klein, "La

théorie de l'expression figurée dans les traités italiens sur les Imprese, 1555–1612," *Bibliothèque d'Humanisme et Renaissance,* 19 (1957), 320.

30. M. Channing Linthicum, *Costume in the Drama of Shakespeare and His Contemporaries* (Oxford: Clarendon Press, 1936), pp. 38–39.

31. *English Emblem Books,* p. 77.

32. Ripa, *Iconologia* (1603), p. 416.

33. Roy Strong, *Portraits of Queen Elizabeth I* (Oxford: Clarendon Press, 1963), p. 121, Plates IX, XI, XVII.

34. Ibid., pp. 111, 129.

35. Roy Strong, *The Elizabethan Image* (London: The Tate Gallery, 1969), p. 12.

36. Cf. Peacham's comments on this emblem in *The Compleat Gentleman,* p. 42.

37. The rose and thistle were traditional heraldic flowers of England and Scotland, and James customarily used them in conjunction as a sign of union.

38. *Emblematum Liber* (1531), sig. A2^v.

39. *The Duty of All True Subjects,* sig. A2^r.

40. Peacham's explanation is modelled on a similar one by Geffrey Whitney in *A Choice of Emblemes* (1586), sig. **3^v. Peacham's "private friendes" who received dedications are Adam Newton, John Dowland, William Stallenge, and Christopher and Mabel Collard.

41. In those emblems copied from Ripa's *Iconologia* (see below) Peacham was also careful not to reverse his originals (the emblem on Matrimony is an exception), since in iconography right and left can have strongly opposed symbolic meanings.

42. Peacham's debt to Ripa has been commented upon by Paul Reyher in *Les Masques Anglais* (Paris: Hachette et Cie., 1909), p. 401; by Freeman in *English Emblem Books,* pp. 79–81; and by Gilbert in *Symbolic Persons,* p. 271. Professor Gilbert at one time planned to make a study of this subject and I am grateful to him for permission to read the preliminary notes that he made. The page numbers of the relevant emblems in *Minerva Britanna* are as follows with the corresponding page numbers of the 1603 edition of Ripa in parentheses: 21 (190), 22 (427), 23 (442), 25 (155), 26 (sig. Hl^r), 46 (388), 47 (229), 126 (79), 127 (77), 128 (75), 129 (78), 132 (306), 134 (500), 141 (140), 146 (383), 147 (225), 149 (49), 153 (466), 206 (147–48).

43. The title page of the Padua, 1611, edition mentioned that the book would be useful also to "Formatori d'Emblemi, & d'Imprese."

44. *Iconologia,* p. 428.

45. Giovio, *Dialogo dell'Imprese* (Lyons, 1559), p. 49; *Minerva Britanna,* p. 106.

46. *A Choice of Emblemes,* pp. 132–33; Alciati, *Emblemata* (Lyons, 1550), No. 195. Alciati had employed a different version in the 1531 edition.

47. The "De Morte et Amore" theme became very popular among Re-

naissance writers. See Joseph G. Fucilla, "De Morte et Amore," *Philological Quarterly,* 14 (1935), 97–104.

48. Sig. A3ʳ. Cf. his reference (p. 90) to having seen the Henry VII impresa in the stained glass of Westminster Abbey.

49. Camden mentions the impresas of Henry VII (p. 163), Sidney (p. 165), and Essex (p. 166), all of which are in Peacham. Camden may also have been the source for Peacham's "Fatum subscribat Eliza" (*Minerva Britanna,* p. 14). Daniel's collection includes the impresa of Carlo Ursino (sig. H3ᵛ); cf. *Minerva Britanna,* p. 113.

50. *English Emblem Books,* p. 81.

51. *Faerie Queene,* I.i.7.

52. Ernst Th. Sehrt, "Der Wald des Irrtums: zur allegorischen Funktion von Spensers *Faerie Queene* I, 7–9," *Anglia,* 86 (1968), 491. Cf. Thomas Warton's edition of Milton's *Poems Upon Several Occasions* (1785), p. 106.

53. *Thalia's Banquet* (1620), sig. A3ʳ.

54. Ibid., Ep. 70. See also the four emblems in *The Period of Mourning* (1613) and the prefatory emblem in *A True Relation* (1615).

55. For a discussion of the provenance and date of this manuscript, see my introduction to the facsimile edition, *Emblemata Varia* (Ilkley and London, 1976).

56. pp. 185–87. Cf. *The More the Merrier* (1608), Ep. 33.

57. *Epistles,* I. xvi. 5–7.

58. The work was not included in Freeman's bibliography of English emblem books and was not generally known to scholars until its recent publication in facsimile.

59. *English Emblem Books,* p. 69.

Chapter Three

1. *The Art of Drawing,* sig. A4ʳ.

2. During the seventeenth century sections of it were considered sufficiently important to be copied out by hand (Bodleian Library: MS Rawlinson B 32, fols. 2–5, 17–38; and British Library: Add. MS 34120, fols. 34–41, and MS Harleian 1279, fol. 12ᵇ). The scribe of MS Harl. 1279 even wrote a reminder to himself (fol. 60ᵇ) to send for a copy of Peacham's book. F. J. Levy is one of the few modern art historians to give the work its due in his "Henry Peacham and the Art of Drawing," *Journal of the Warburg and Courtauld Institute,* 37 (1974), 174–90.

3. *Graphice,* sig. A3ʳ.

4. *The Art of Drawing,* sig. A3ᵛ.

5. *The Book named The Governor,* ed. S. E. Lehmberg (London: Dent, 1962), pp. 23–26.

6. Lawrence Stone, *The Crisis of the Aristocracy* (Oxford: Clarendon Press, 1965), p. 680.

7. Chapter V, p. 22.

8. *Queene Elizabethes Achademy* (British Library: MS Lansdowne 98, art 1), ed. F. J. Furnivall for The Early English Text Society, Extra Series, No. VIII (London: Trubner, 1869), p. 1.

9. *Thalia's Banquet*, Ep. 70.

10. Nicholas Hilliard, "A Treatise Concerning the Arte of Limning," ed. Philip Norman, *Walpole Society*, 1 (1911–12), 15–45. In his introduction Norman disclaims any influence upon Peacham by Hilliard: "H. Peacham's *Art of drawing with the pen and limming in water colours*, although commending Hilliard, seems independent of him" (p. 11).

11. *The Book of the Courtier*, trans. Sir Thomas Hoby (London, 1928), p. 77. Cf. *Graphice*, p. 3, and *The Compleat Gentleman*, p. 106.

12. Haydocke, *A Tracte Containing the Artes of Curious Paintinge*, pp. 3–4, 152. On this point see John Pope-Hennessy's "Nicholas Hilliard and Mannerist Art Theory," *Journal of the Warburg and Courtauld Institute*, 6 (1943), 90.

13. *The Art of Drawing*, pp. 7–8, 20–21, 26–27, 29, 30–31, 63–65, 69–70.

14. Peacham's definitions of "shadow" and of primary and secondary light (p. 30) are paraphrased from Lomazzo's *Artes of Curious Paintinge*, pp. 140, 142.

15. I am grateful to Professor Allan Gilbert of Duke University for first pointing out to me Peacham's use of Ripa in *Graphice*.

16. " 'Has been,' 'shall be,' and 'was' exist no more,/ But 'is' and 'now,' 'the present' and 'today,'/ 'Eternity' alone, one and complete" (Ernest Hatch Wilkins, trans., in *The Triumphs of Petrarch* [Chicago: University of Chicago Press, 1962], p. 110).

17. *Graphice*, p. 111; Ripa, *Iconologia*, p. 483: "Hvomo vecchio alato, [. . .] & stà in mezzo d'vna ruina, hà la bocca aperta, mostrando i denti, li quali sieno del colore del ferro."

18. *The Queenes Achademy*, p. 8; cf. Ruth Kelso, *The Doctrine of the English Gentleman in the Sixteenth Century* (Urbana, 1929), p. 141.

19. MS Harleian 1500. This work consists of twenty-six documents. Two on fol. 116^b are signed and twenty others are in a similar hand.

20. See pp. 147, 148, 150. Peacham's pages on color and light owe something to Lomazzo's chapter "Of the Effects which Light Cavseth in Colovrs."

21. Sig. A3^r. For the presumed date of this meeting, see Chapter 1 above.

22. For a fuller discussion of the term, see John E. Mason, *Gentlefolk in the Making* (Philadelphia, 1935), p. 4.

23. Ibid., p. 4.

24. See especially Kelso's chapter on "What is a Gentleman?" in *The Doctrine of the English Gentleman*.

25. On the degree to which courtesy literature addressed ostensibly to the gentry was familiar to citizens of a lower social status, see Louis B.

Wright, *Middle-Class Culture in Elizabethan England* (1935; rpt. Ithaca, New York: Cornell University Press, 1958), pp. 123–24, 126.

26. On this matter, see Mason, *Gentlefolk in the Making*, pp. 46–47, and Kelso, *The Doctrine of the English Gentleman*, pp. 19–41.

27. Bk. IV, ch. 3, p. 134. Cf. Elyot, *The Book named The Governor*, p. 42.

28. Cf. Roger Ascham's complaint in *The Scholemaster*, ed. Edward Arber (Boston: Heath, 1898), pp. 51, 174.

29. Peacham's statement is borrowed directly from Elyot's *The Governor*, p. 44.

30. For a summary of English Humanist views on the education of the young, see Pearl Hogrefe, *The Sir Thomas More Circle* (Urbana: University of Illinois Press, 1959), pp. 140–200.

31. For a discussion of the views of Erasmus and Vives concerning this matter, see William Harrison Woodward's *Studies in Education during the Age of the Renaissance* (Cambridge: Cambridge University Press, 1924), pp. 119, 193.

32. Stone, *The Crisis of the Aristocracy*, p. 689.

33. Ascham's text deals in Book I with "The Bringing up of Youth" and in Book II with "The Ready Way to the Latin Tongue."

34. *The Governor*, p. 18.

35. J. W. H. Atkins, *English Literary Criticism: The Renascence* (London: Methuen, 1947), p. 294.

36. Peacham's borrowings from Puttenham (ed. G. Gregory Smith, *Elizabethan Critical Essays*, Vol. II [Oxford: Oxford University Press, 1904]) and from Scaliger are as follows: p. 79 (Puttenham, p. 6); pp. 81–82 (Puttenham, pp. 17, 21); pp. 82–87 (Scaliger III, 24–26); pp. 87–88 (Scaliger VI, 7); pp. 89–90 (Scaliger VI, 5–7); p. 90 (Scaliger VI, 2); pp. 94–96 (Puttenham, pp. 61–66). Certain divergences from Puttenham are noted by Edith A. Palmer in "George Puttenham and Henry Peacham: Copia and Decorum in Sixteenth Century Literature," MPhil. thesis, London University 1969, pp. 26–37.

37. Cf. *The Civile Conversation*, trans. George Pettie, 1581 (London: Constable, 1925), I, 206; *Thalia's Banquet*, Ep. 38; *The Truth of Our Times*, sig. C6^{r-v}.

38. The anecdote is taken from an entry under "1581" in Surius's *Commentario Brevis Rerum in Orbe Salutis* (1586 ed.), pp. 1026–27.

39. Cf. the equally technical comments he makes on Orazio Vecchi's Canzonets (p. 102).

40. Peacham's description of a Bellini painting and his story of an Antwerp blacksmith (p. 117) then follow. These were copied out by an unknown seventeenth-century writer in his notes on "The art of Painting in Oyle" (British Library: MS Sloane 1448.b.) together with other parts of the relevant chapter in *The Compleat Gentleman*.

41. Peacham's achievement in this matter has not been recognized, and it appears to be commonly believed that the first English translation was by William Aglionby in 1685. But see Levy's "Henry Peacham and the Art of Drawing," and Luigi Salerno, "Seventeenth Century English Literature on Painting," *Journal of the Warburg and Courtauld Institute,* 14 (1951), 237.

42. *Het Leven Der Moderne oft dees-tijtsche doorluchtighe Italiensche Schilders* (1604) provided a shortened version of Vasari, and Peacham in turn further condenses and selects. Twelve of Peacham's lives derive (via Van Mander) from Part One of Vasari's 1568 edition (i.e., that part dealing with the Trecento), five lives come from Part Two (the Quattrocento), and only one life (Raphael) is taken from Part Three (the Cinquecento).

43. The following are from *A Display of Heraldrie,* the page numbers of which are given in parentheses: pp. 159 (241), 162 (87), 163 (158), 165 (148), 166 (141), 167 (243), 172 (168), 173 (105).

44. *The Scholemaster,* pp. 133–34; *The Governor,* pp. 77–88; *Positions,* Ch. 16, p. 75; *Queene Elizabethes Achademy,* p. 7; Cleland, *Institution,* Bk. V, ch. 23, pp. 225–26.

45. Ascham's warnings about Italy are well known. Cf. William Rankins's *The English Ape* (1588); Thomas Nashe's *Pierce Pennilesse* (1592); and Joseph Hall's *Quo Vadis? A Just Censure of Travell* (1617).

46. Stone, *The Crisis of the Aristocracy,* p. 693.

47. *Bibliotheca Lindesiana* (Aberdeen: Aberdeen University Press, 1910), III, col. 6923. I have been unable to trace this copy of Peacham's book.

48. W. C. Hazlitt, *Collections and Notes* (London: Reeves and Turner, 1876), p. 324.

49. I have been unable to trace this copy.

50. Peacham adjusts his text to take account of the recent deaths of the Earl of Dorset and Sir Henry Hobart, and he adds references to the Countesses of Nottingham and Holdernes, to the Cary family, and to "my worthy friend M. *Edward Riuers* Marchant" (p. 185).

51. Cf. Leonard Mascall, *A Booke of Fishing* (1590), John Taverner, *Certaine experiments concerning fish and fruite* (1600), John Dennys, *The secrets of angling* (1613), Gervase Markham, *The pleasures of princes* (1614).

52. Such changes may, of course, have been made by the printer rather than Peacham.

53. The second of these chapters must have been a late addition. Though listed in the table of contents as Chap. 14, it appears neither in the British Library copy (British Library: 16575) nor in the Bodleian Library copy (Art 4° P49) in which the chapter "Of Armory or Blazon of Armes" appears instead numbered as Chapter XIV. Those copies containing the new chapter (e.g., British Library: 721. e. 17) have three extra leaves inserted (X4, X5, X6).

54. Those copies with engraved title pages (e.g., Bodleian Library: Douce PP 233) continue to use the same plate as was originally used for the first two editions, but, as in the case of the second edition, an alteration is made to the date (now "Anno 1634"). The date of the engraving itself is left alone ("Sculp. Anno 1626"), and, more surprisingly, the words "The second Impression much Inlarged" also remain, thereby providing a source for future error in the form of the words "The Third Impression much enlarged" that appear on the title page of the 1661 edition.

55. "Changing Ideals of Aristocratic Character and Conduct in Seventeenth Century England," *Modern Philology*, 30 (1932–33), 154; Brathwaite, *The English Gentleman*, sig. ¶2ʳ. Though Brathwaite's opinions are often puritanical in character, he himself was not a Puritan as is clear from certain denunciations of Puritanism in the book.

Chapter Four

1. Epistle to the Reader, sig. A3ᵛ.

2. *The More the Merrier* was formerly attributed to Henry Parrot, but Margaret C. Pitman showed that this was not so in her M.A. thesis ("Studies in the Works of Henry Peacham," London University, 1933, pp. 200–03). Cf. Pitman's "The Epigrams of Henry Peacham and Henry Parrot," *Modern Language Review*, 29 (1934), 129–36.

3. E.g. *Minerva Britanna*, pp. 185–87; *Thalia's Banquet*, Ep. 80.

4. Ruth Wallerstein, *Studies in Seventeenth-Century Poetic* (Madison, Wisc.: University of Wisconsin Press, 1950), p. 26. Robert R. Cawley in *Henry Peacham: His Contribution to English Poetry* (University Park, Pa., 1971) treats the verses of *Minerva Britanna* as though they were a collection of epigrams.

5. Francis Weitzmann, "Notes on the Elizabethan *Elegie*," *Publications of the Modern Language Society of America*, 50 (1935), 435–43.

6. Wallerstein, *Studies in Seventeenth-Century Poetic*, pp. 5, 59–95; and Cawley, *Henry Peacham*, p. 76.

7. *The Works of Francis Bacon*, eds. James Spedding, Robert L. Ellis, and Douglas D. Heath (London: Longman, 1858), VI, 329, 328.

8. *Henry Peacham*, pp. 92–95.

9. Ibid., p. 95. The influence of Spenser on Peacham was remarked upon in several notes by the editor of the 1789 edition of *The Period of Mourning* (pp. 7, 41, 42). These were reprinted in Francis G. Waldron's edition in *The Literary Museum* (1792). Earlier Waldron had argued in an "Appendix" to his edition of Ben Jonson's *The Sad Shepherd* (1783) that "A Vision Upon this his Minerva," signed E. S. in *Minerva Britanna*, was by Spenser (pp. 144–50), and he repeated his rather unconvincing argument in *The Literary Museum* (pp. 9–12).

10. Cawley, *Henry Peacham*, p. 84.

11. As Peacham was aware, Henry was a fine horseman and had a great love of riding.

12. There is some typical self-advertisement here, "COMPLEMENT" being an allusion to the passage on Sackville in *The Compleat Gentleman*, as a marginal note explains.

13. *The Compleat Gentleman*, pp. 191, 192.

14. "The Country House Poem of the Seventeenth Century," *Journal of the Warburg and Courtauld Institute*, 19 (1956), 164.

15. Cawley, *Henry Peacham*, p. 105.

16. Peacham was clearly proud of these lines, and he quoted them, in slightly altered form, in *Coach and Sedan*, sig. D3^r.

17. Cf. *Aeneid*, Bk. XI, 67–70.

18. The 1789 editor of the poem compared Peacham's enumeration of the sea-nymphs to Spenser's *Faerie Queene*, IV.xi.48ff.

19. "Studies in Henry Peacham," p. 175.

20. *Thalia's Banquet*, Ep. 30.

Chapter Five

1. The work was entered in the Stationer's Register on 9 February, 1635/36, and its dedication is dated 19 February, 1636.

2. Cf. the "Proclamation for the Restraint of Excessiue Carriages" (9 March, 1629); the "Proclamation for the Restraint of Excessive Carriages to the Destruction of the Highways" (1 Nov., 1635); and John Taylor's *Life of Thomas Parr* (1635) in *Works of John Taylor the Water Poet*, Publications of the Spenser Society, Issue No. 7 (1870), sig. D4^r.

3. The author-narrator at one point recounts the story (quoted above from *The Worth of a Peny*) of the Cambridge scholars who lacked sufficient payment for their puddings. The Vicar is identified as the bold one who discovered the needed penny inside the pudding, and Peacham is identified as one of his companions in the episode.

4. The village of Wrangle is close to Leverton, and Peacham obviously knew it well (see p. 6).

5. "The Compte and seuerall Answeres of Henry Peacham Clarke and Richard Peacham Gent," PRO: Chancery Proceedings: Hawerdon vs. Peacham 1618, C. 2. James I. H. 16. 12.

6. *Henry Peacham: His Contribution to English Poetry* (University Park, Pa., 1971), p. 15; cf. Cawley's introduction to the facsimile edition of *The Truth of Our Times* (New York, 1942).

7. Pancirolli's work was first written in Italian but did not appear in print until Henry Salmuth translated the original into Latin in 1599 and added copious annotations. In 1607, the original manuscript being lost, an Italian version was produced from the Latin text. From a marginal annotation on page 53, it is clear that Peacham worked from a Latin edition.

Peacham usually translates Pancirolli word for word but selects and paraphrases Salmuth's annotations.

8. Other sources appear to include such writers as Pliny, Tacitus,
Galen, and Camden.

9. The popularity of *The Worth of a Peny* may have led to an eight-page
pirate edition which appeared anonymously in 1642 as *A CAVTION TO
KEEPE MONEY: Showing the Miserie of the want thereof*. It is much
shorter than *The Worth of a Peny*, its wording is frequently very different,
its contents are arranged in a different sequence, it omits all cautionary
discussion of thrift, and it contains material not found in the longer work.
Margaret C. Pitman, who was the first to note the debts to *The Worth of a
Peny*, claims that *A Caution to Keepe Money* "almost certainly represents
Peacham's first draft of the full length pamphlet" ("Studies in the Works of
Henry Peacham," M.A. thesis, London University, 1933, p. 267. Cf. p. 69).

10. The book was entered in the Stationer's Register on 13 April, 1639,
and its dedication "To all his Maiesties Loyall and Trve loving Subjects" is
dated 7 May, 1639.

11. Peacham signed this work, which was not entered in the Stationer's
Register, with the anagram "Ryhen Pameach."

12. Abbots's work first was originally composed, as its title page explains,
in 1600 as a protest against the rebuilding of the cross.

13. See, for example, the anonymous *A Resolution of the Roundheads to
Pull down Cheapside Crosse* (1641); and *A Dolefull Lamentation of Cheapside Crosse* (1641). Peacham himself had earlier discussed Puritan attitudes
to representations of the Cross in *Graphice*, pp. 13–14.

14. This representation of Cheapside Cross was later imitated on the title
page of the anonymous *The Downe-fall of Dagon, or the taking downe of
Cheape-side Crosse* (1643), a work which borrows and paraphrases much of
Peacham's text.

15. *The Remarkable Funeral of Cheapside-Crosse in London* (1642), sig.
A2^r.

16. See Richard Overton's *Articles of High Treason Exhibited Against
Cheap-Side Crosse* (1642); *The Remarkable Funeral of Cheap-Side Crosse*
(1642); *An Answer to the Lamentation of Cheapside Crosse* (1642); *The
Crosses Case in Cheapside* (1642); and *Cheapside Crosse Censured and
Condemned* (1643).

17. Samuel R. Gardiner, *History of the Great Civil War 1642–1649*
(London: Longmans and Co., 1893), I, 132; and W. K. Jordan, *The Development of Religious Toleration in England* (London: Allen and Unwin
1938), III, 43.

18. But see Harold P. Levitt's "The Political Writings of Henry
Peacham," Diss. New York University, 1968.

19. The precise date of Milton's pamphlet and its place in the sequence is
not absolutely certain, and I am here accepting the suggested date given by

Rudolph Kirk and William P. Baker in *Complete Prose Works of John Milton* (New Haven: Yale University Press, 1953), I, 653.

20. The title page of the work is signed "H. P." That the work is by Peacham seems clear from anecdotes he had earlier employed elsewhere and from the way in which the autobiographical information he supplies fits in with what we already know about him.

21. In the text the woodcut is referred to by Time as "an *Embleme* of the Revolution and Change of these Present times" (p. 2).

22. *Complete Prose Works*, I, 972.

23. *The Works of the Right Reverend Joseph Hall, D.D.*, ed. Philip Wynter (Oxford: Oxford University Press, 1863), IX, 369, 370.

24. Enigmatically, Peacham concludes by saying: "but the Master-peece of his bountie I must conceale." Presumably Williams had done him some great personal service.

Selected Bibliography

PRIMARY SOURCES

1. Manuscripts *(in chronological order)*

1595 Drawing of a Scene from Shakespeare's *Titus Andronicus*. Signed "Henricus Peacham." Harley Papers, Vol. I, fol. 159^b.

1603 Madrigal "Awake softly with singing Oriana sleeping." Undated. Signed "Henry Pecham." British Library: MS Harleian 6855, Art. 13.

1603–04 "ΒΑΣΙΛΙΚΟΝ ΔΩΡΟΝ In Heroica Emblemata." Emblem book with pen and ink drawings. Dedicated to Prince Henry. Undated. Signed "Henricum Peachamum." Bodleian Library: MS Rawlinson poetry 146.

1604 "ΒΑΣΙΛΙΚΟΝ ΔΩΡΟΝ ΕΙΣ ΤΑ ΕΜΒΛΗΜΑΤΑ ΒΑΣΙΛΙΚΑ." Emblem book with pen and ink drawings. Dedicated to James I. Undated. Signed "Henrico Pechamo." British Museum: MS Harleian 6855, Art. 13.

1610 "ΒΑΣΙΛΙΚΟΝ ΔΩΡΟΝ IN BASILICA EMBLEMATA." Emblem book with water color illustrations. Undated. Signed "Henrico Peachamo." British Library: MS Royal 12A LXVI.

1612 Frontispiece portrait of Prince Henry in water colors for James Cleland's "Le Povrtraict de Monseigneur le Prince." Dated London, 1612. Signed "Henr: Peacham f." British Library: MS Royal 16E XXXVIII.

1621–22 "Emblemata Varia." Emblem book with pen and ink drawings. Dedicated to Sir Julius Caesar. Undated. Signed "Henricus Peacham." Folger Shakespeare Library: MS. V. b. 45.

Date uncertain. Heraldic notes on Cater family. Two signed by Henry Peacham. British Library: MS Harleian 1500.

Date uncertain. "Travellers on the Road." Pen and india ink wash drawing. Attributed (probably in error) to Peacham in *Catalogue of an Exhibition of the Works of British-Born Artists of the Seventeenth Century* (London: Burlington Fine Arts Club, 1938), item 107. Signed "HP. F." Courtauld Institute: Witt Bequest.

Date uncertain. "Travellers at a Village." Pen and india ink wash drawing. Attributed (probably in error) to Peacham in *Catalogue of an Exhibi-*

tion of the Works of British-Born Artists of the Seventeenth Century,
item 106. Present location unknown.

2. Printed *(in chronological order of first publication)*
The Art of Drawing with the Pen, and Limming in Water Colovrs. 1606.
————another issue with cancelled title-page. 1607.
————facsimile of 1606 edition. The English Experience No. 230. Amster-
dam: Theatrum Orbis Terrarum, 1970.
"Ad Robertum Doulandum." Dedicatory poem in Robert Dowland's *A
Musical Banquet.* 1610.
"Vpon the Authour and his most commendable and necessary worke."
Dedicatory poem in Arthur Standish's *The Commons Complaint.* 1611.
"Memoriae Sacrum." Poem in Thomas Coryate's *Coryats Crudities.*
1611.
"To the famous Traveller." Dedicatory poem in *Coryats Crudities.*
"In the Vtopian tongue." Poem in *Coryats Crudities.*
Minerva Britanna or A Garden of Heroical Deuises. 1612.
————facsimile edition. Leeds: Scolar Press, 1966.
————facsimile edition. Introduction by John Horden. Menston: Scolar
Press, 1969 (reprinted 1973).
————facsimile edition. The English Experience No. 407. Amsterdam:
Theatrum Orbis Terrarum, 1971.
Graphice or The Most Avncient and Excellent Art of Drawing and Limming.
1612.
————another issue with cancelled title page. *The Gentleman's Exercise or
An Exquisite Practice.* 1612.
————*The Gentleman's Exercise.* 1634. (Also issued as Part II of *The Com-
pleat Gentleman.* 1634.)
     The Gentleman's Exercise. 1661. (Published as Part II of *The Com-
pleat Gentleman.* 1661.)
*The Period of Mourning. Disposed into Six Visions. In Memorie of the Late
Prince. Together with Nuptiall Hymnes.* 1613.
————another issue with cancelled title page as H4. 1613; 1789.
————reprinted by F. G. Waldron in *The Literary Museum.* 1792.
*Prince Henrie Revived. Or A Poeme Vpon the Birth, and in Honor of the
Hopefull Yong Prince Henrie Frederick.* 1615.
*The More the Merrier. Containing: Threescore and Odde Headlesse Epi-
grams.* 1608.
A Most Trve Relation of the Affaires of Cleve and Gvlick. 1615.
————facsimile edition. The English Experience No. 549. Amsterdam:
Theatrum Orbis Terrarum, 1973.
*Thalia's Banquet: Furnished with an Hundred and Odde Dishes of Newly
Deuised Epigrammes.* 1620.

The Compleat Gentleman Furnishing Him Absolute in the Most Necessary and Commendable Qualities. 1622, 1627, 1634, 1661.

————*Peacham's Compleat Gentleman 1634*. Introduction by G. S. Gordon. Oxford: Clarendon Press, 1906.

————*The Complete Gentleman*. Ed. Virgil B. Heltzel. Ithaca: Cornell University Press, 1962.

————facsimile of 1622 edition. The English Experience No. 59. Amsterdam: Theatrum Orbis Terrarum, 1968.

An Aprill Shower Shed in Abundance of Teares. 1624.

Thestylis Atrata: Or A Funeral Elegie. 1634.

Coach and Sedan, Pleasantly Disputing for Place and Precedence. 1636.

————reprinted from edition of 1636. London: Printed for Frederick Etchells and Hugh Macdonald, 1925.

"Graenwich." Verses for engraving by Wenceslaus Hollar. 1637.

"Seleucus and Son." Verses for engraving by Hollar. 1637.

The Valley of Varietie: Or, Discourse fitting for the Times. 1638.

The Truth of Our Times: Revealed out of One Mans Experience. 1638.

————facsimile edition. Introduction by Robert R. Cawley. New York: Columbia University Press, 1942.

————Ed. Vergil B. Heltzel. With *The Complete Gentleman*. Ithaca: Cornell University Press, 1962.

"Richard II. Virgin and Child." Verses for engraving by Hollar. 1639.

A Merry Discovrse of Mevm, and Tvvm. 1639.

The Dvty of All Trve Svbiects to Their King. 1639.

The Worth of a Peny: Or, A Caution to Keep Money. 1641.

————another issue with cancelled title page. 1647.

————other editions. 1664, 1667, 1669, 1677, 1686, 1687, 1695, 1704.

————in Edward Arber's *An English Garner*. Birmingham, 1883. VI, 245–73.

————in Edward Arber's *An English Garner. Social England Illustrated*. New introduction by Andrew Lang. Westminster: Constable, 1903. Pp. 363–406.

"En Surculus Arbor." Verses for engraving by Hollar. 1641.

A Dialogue between the Crosse in Cheap, and Charing Crosse. 1641.

"The World is Ruled and Governed by Opinion." Verses for engraving by Hollar. [?1641–42.]

The Art of Living in London. 1642.

————Ed. Vergil B. Heltzel. With *The Complete Gentleman*. Ithaca: Cornell University Press, 1962.

A Paradox, in the Praise of a Dunce, to Smectymnuus. 1642.

Square-Caps Turned intò Rovnd-Heads. 1642.

"Royal Exchange." Verses for engraving by Hollar. 1644.

"Emblemata Varia." Facsimile edition, with introduction by Alan R. Young. Ilkley and London: Scolar Press, 1976.

SELECTED SECONDARY SOURCES

BESLY, JOHN. "Malone's Own Notes in Copies of Peacham's Various Publications." *Notes and Queries*. 1st Ser. 9 (1855), 218. Discusses Malone's annotations in Bodleian Library copies of Peacham. Some helpful biographical speculation. This article is preceded by an unsigned note containing a letter from Thomas Part to Malone on the subject of Peacham's biography.

CAWLEY, ROBERT R. *Henry Peacham: His Contribution to English Poetry*. University Park: Pennsylvania State University Press, 1971. A brief biography (based on Pitman's thesis) and detailed consideration of poetry. Good on placing epigrams and elegies in context of literary tradition.

————. Introduction to facsimile edition of *The Truth of Our Times*. New York: Columbia University Press, 1942. Pp. v-xxiii. Convincingly calls attention to merits of this attractive work.

CHAMBERS, EDMUND K. "The First Illustration to 'Shakespeare'." *The Library*. 4th Ser. 5(1925), 326–30, Plate XI. The first recognition of the importance of Peacham's drawing of a scene from *Titus Andronicus*.

CLARK, JAMES D. "Henry Peacham's *Minerva Britanna* (1612): A Bibliographical Description and Analysis." M.A. Thesis. University of Leeds, 1977. Provides a detailed analysis of the manner and production of Peacham's emblem book and discusses the significance of the bibliographical variants among extant copies.

FREEMAN, ROSEMARY. *English Emblem Books*. London: Chatto and Windus, 1948. Assesses Peacham's contribution to emblem literature. Notes influence of Spenser and Ripa.

GILBERT, ALLAN H. *The Symbolic Persons in the Masques of Ben Jonson*. Durham, N. Carolina: Duke University Press, 1948. Brief discussion of *Minerva Britanna*. Notes debt to Ripa.

GORDON, G. S. Introduction to *Peacham's Compleat Gentleman 1634*. Oxford: Clarendon Press, 1906. Pp. v-xxiii. Stresses "Cavalier" aspects of *Compleat Gentleman*. Helpful on tradition of courtesy literature. Inaccurate on biography.

HELTZEL, VIRGIL B. Introductions to combined edition of *The Complete Gentleman, The Truth of Our Times, and The Art of Living in London*. Ithaca: Cornell University Press, 1962. Pp. ix-xx. Chiefly on *Compleat Gentleman*. Briefly relates it to courtesy literature.

HORDEN, JOHN. Introduction to facsimile edition of *Minerva Britanna*. Menston: Scolar Press, 1969. Reprinted 1973. 3 pp. (unpaginated). Concise assessment of Peacham's contribution to emblem literature.

KELSO, RUTH. *The Doctrine of the English Gentleman in the Sixteenth Century.* University of Illinois Studies in Language and Literature, No. 14. Urbana, Illinois: University of Illinois Press, 1929. Discusses *Compleat Gentleman* and relationship to courtesy literature.

L[EE], S[IDNEY]. "Henry Peacham." *The Dictionary of National Biography.* London: Oxford University Press, 1921–22. XV, 578–80. Includes a number of inaccuracies which are discussed in detail in Margaret Pitman's M.A. thesis.

LEVITT, HAROLD P. "The Political Writings of Henry Peacham." Diss. New York University, 1968. Concentrates on late pamphlets and tracts. Connects Peacham with Smectymnuus debate.

LEVY, F. J. "Henry Peacham and the Art of Drawing." *Journal of the Warburg and Courtauld Institute*, 37 (1974), 174–90. Useful assessment of Peacham's contribution to writings on art.

LIEVESAY, JOHN L. *Stefano Guazzo and the English Renaissance.* Chapel Hill: University of N. Carolina Press, 1961. Discusses influence of Guazzo on *Compleat Gentleman* and *Thalia's Banquet* (pp. 244–47).

MASON, JOHN E. *Gentlefolk in the Making: Studies in the History of English Courtesy Literature and Related Topics from 1531 to 1774.* Philadelphia: University of Pennsylvania Press, 1935. Discusses *Compleat Gentleman* and relationship to courtesy literature.

PALMER, EDITH ANNETTE. "George Puttenham and Henry Peacham: Copia and Decorum in Sixteenth Century Literature." MPhil. Thesis. London University, 1969. Discusses *The Compleat Gentleman* and Peacham's views on literary style.

PITMAN, MARGARET C. "The Epigrams of Henry Peacham and Henry Parrot." *Modern Language Review*, 29 (1934), 129–36. Establishes respective authorship of collections of epigrams by two writers.

————. "Studies in the Works of Henry Peacham." M.A. Thesis. London University, 1933. A major contribution to the study of Peacham. Particularly important for biographical and bibliographical findings.

————. "Summaries of Theses: No. CXVI." *Bulletin of the Institute of Historical Research*, 11 (1933), 189–92. Valuable summary of the findings of her M.A. thesis.

RIMBAULT, EDWARD F. "Autobiographical Notices of Henry Peacham." *Notes and Queries.* 3rd Ser. 12 (1867), 221–22. Cites several autobiographical passages in Peacham's writings.

SCHOENBAUM, SAMUEL. *William Shakespeare: A Documentary Life.* Oxford: Clarendon Press, 1975. Helpful summary of current scholarly assessments of Peacham's *Titus Andronicus* drawing.

STARNES, D. T. "Elyot's 'Governour' and Peacham's 'Compleat Gentleman'." *Modern Language Review*, 22 (1927), 319–22. Comments on Peacham's debt to Elyot in *Compleat Gentleman*.

STRONG, ROY C. "Elizabeth I as Oriana." *SRen*, 6 (1959), 251–60. Includes brief discussion of Peacham's madrigal.

THOMPSON, E.N.S. *Literary By Paths of the Renaissance*. New Haven: Yale University Press, 1924. Helpful introductory chapters on emblem books and courtesy literature both of which refer to Peacham.

WILSON, ELKIN C. *Prince Henry and English Literature*. Ithaca: Cornell University Press, 1946. Discusses Peacham's relationship with Prince Henry and the works dedicated to him.

WILSON, JOHN DOVER. "*Titus Andronicus* on the Stage in 1595." *Shakespeare Survey*, 1 (1948), 17–22. Accords Peacham's drawing great importance among extant documents relating to Elizabethan theater.

YOUNG, ALAN R. Introduction to facsimile of *Emblemata Varia*. Ilkley and London: Scolar Press, 1976. 9 pp. (unpaginated). The first detailed account of the manuscript. Also includes some new biographical details.

————. "A Biographical Note on Henry Peacham." *Notes and Queries*, New Series, 24 (1977), 214–17. Discusses Peacham's teaching activities, his marriage, and his last years.

————. "Henry Peacham, Author of *The Garden of Eloquence* (1577): A Biographical Note." *Notes and Queries*, New Series, 24 (1977), 503–07. A brief biography of Peacham's father.

Index

DATE DUE

GAYLORD   PRINTED IN U.S.A